FRANK LLOYD WRIGHT IN THE MOVIES

FRANK LLOYD WRIGHT IN THE MOVIES

ICONIC CALIFORNIA SITES ON FILM

MARK ANTHONY WILSON

WITH PHOTOGRAPHY BY JOEL PULIAITTI | FOREWORD BY MARC WANAMAKER

Published by The History Press
An imprint of Arcadia Publishing
Charleston, SC
www.historypress.com

Front cover, top: Scene from the 1959 movie *House on Haunted Hill*, with guests arriving at the Ennis House; *bottom*: Marin County Civic Center, Administration Building, 1959–1962. *Photo by Joel Puliatti.*
Back cover: Living room of the Walker House, Carmel, used as a setting in *A Summer Place*. *Photo by Joel Puliatti.*

First published 2025
Updated November 2025

Manufactured in the United States

ISBN 9781467159555

Library of Congress Control Number: 2025935712

Notice: The information in this book is true and complete to the best of our knowledge. It is offered without guarantee on the part of the author or The History Press. The author and The History Press disclaim all liability in connection with the use of this book.

This book is dedicated to my brother, John "J.B." Wilson,
film historian extraordinaire;
And to my friend Amanda Solar, who has always believed in my writing.

BOOKS BY MARK ANTHONY WILSON

East Bay Heritage: A Potpourri of Living History (1979)
A Living Legacy: Historic Architecture of the East Bay (1987)
Julia Morgan: Architect of Beauty (2007)
Bernard Maybeck: Architect of Elegance (2011)
Frank Lloyd Wright on the West Coast (2014)
South Side Story: A Novel of Chicago in the Early Sixties (2018)
The Open House Murders: An Offbeat San Francisco Thriller (2019)
The Redlining Murders: A Novel of Suspense, Corruption, and Social Justice (2024)

CONTENTS

CONTENTS

LIST OF MOVIES AND TV SERIES DESCRIBED IN THIS BOOK

MOVIES

Female (1933)
Five (1951)
House on Haunted Hill (1959)
A Summer Place (1959)
THX 1138 (1971)
The Terminal Man (1974)
The Day of the Locust (1975)
Blade Runner (1982)
Karate Kid III (1989)
Black Rain (1989)
Cannibal Women in the Avocado Jungle of Death (1989)
Grand Canyon (1991)
The Rocketeer (1991)
The Glimmer Man (1996)
Gattaca (1997)
The Replacement Killers (1998)
Rush Hour (1998)
Permanent Midnight (1998)
The Thirteenth Floor (1999)
DreamQuil (2025)

TV SERIES

Star Trek: Deep Space Nine (1993–1999)
Westworld (2016–2022)
The Venture Bros. (2003–2018)

Map by Joel Puliatti.

FOREWORD

As a Los Angeles and motion picture historian, I could not help learning how "real" history and motion picture history intertwine. From all my research on the history of the motion picture studios in the United States, I created Bison Archives, a specialized research library on the motion picture industry and the people who created this new art of motion pictures. Being a native of Los Angeles and growing up in the West Hollywood and Beverly Hills area, I was exposed to the history of the area as a young person and visited many historic sites that I later chronicled in the many books and articles I wrote. Over the years, thousands of historic photographs of the Los Angeles area were added to the collection, enriching its research importance, which led to supplying images to over two hundred documentaries, books, magazines, exhibitions, museums, historical societies, and national historic sites. Bison Archives became a consultant to the Los Angeles Conservancy and other groups seeking preservation of public and private historic locations.

Film locations became a central interest of Bison Archives, and through the former studio research libraries, thousands of location photographs were saved from destruction and added to the collection. The film location files cover almost every site, public and private, since the early twentieth century. About this time, the studios had people searching and photographing historic sites as well as the current city itself to be used as backgrounds for outdoor scenes. By the early 1920s, these departments were organized into studio archives used for film production. For more than one hundred years, the Los

Angeles area has been shaped and reshaped to accommodate filmmakers' visions. It has played everything—the old South, Africa, Switzerland, ancient Greece and even outer space.

I was contacted by Mark Anthony Wilson in 2007 about the possibility of using an image of architect Julia Morgan, as I had a unique photograph of Morgan with William Randolph Hearst at Hearst Castle in 1926. Studio art directors were inspired by architects like Julia Morgan. I also provided images from Bison Archives for his later books on architects Bernard Maybeck and Frank Lloyd Wright. So, when Mark contacted me again in 2024 about his new project, I was happy to offer my help by providing images from the films he was planning to include in this book.

The "Hollywood" architectural style was taken from movie settings that were designed by artists and architects who were working at the film studios. The Hollywood and Beverly Hills neighborhoods of Los Angeles reflected architectural styles from around the world. For a long time, the dominant architectural style was Spanish Colonial Revival, with European Baronial, Hacienda and some Art Deco also sprinkled around. By the 1920s, the influence of the film industry on residential design had grown, and many stars, directors and producers hired well-known architects to create unusual homes, with some interiors designed and installed by motion picture studio art departments.

Into this Hollywood architectural culture entered Frank Lloyd Wright. In his long career, Wright designed office buildings, churches, museums, gas stations and around 260 residences. Many of the Hollywood architects considered themselves artists as well as architects. Wright was evolving as an architect/artist, moving with the social trends and changing cultural values, which were reflected in his projects. Wright used new building materials spawned by new technologies, even though they might not prove to be durable in the future. Wright designed homes that fit into their environment, like his beach and desert designs. His buildings were ahead of their time and were employed years later as iconic settings by some of Hollywood's most innovative filmmakers. Wright's designs were fresh and filled with ideas that have inspired studio art directors.

Art direction in films is important to the development of the motion picture industry, as is the influence of architects and interior designers around the world. Frank Lloyd Wright was one of these influencers. To this day, Frank Lloyd Wright attracts attention! Even young people have heard his name. Wright has inspired many books and pop culture references. His work has been seen in motion pictures since the 1930s. Unusual homes like Wright's were often chosen by film studios for exotic locations. Using historical photos the studios provided, production companies were inclined to film in these sites, which gave their movies an authenticity that was sometimes duplicated in the studio itself if the site was not practical to shoot at. One of the more popular Wright houses was the Ennis House in the Los Feliz district of Los Angles. It is a spectacular site in the hills above Hollywood. The Ennis House has long fascinated Hollywood art directors and was an inspiration for the Universal horror classic, *The Black Cat*, in 1934. Also in the Los Feliz district is Wright's Storer House on Hollywood Boulevard, which is a major tourist attraction. In East Hollywood, another iconic Wright site is the Barnsdall "Hollyhock" House, built in 1917 when Hollywood was evolving into a motion picture center.

Since then, these Wright landmarks have been seen as Hollywood settings or artworks more than residences. Frank Lloyd Wright houses are very cinematic and theatrical in their designs. They were perfect film locations, fascinating audiences, and have been tourist destinations for years. This publication in Mark's book of film locations using Frank Lloyd Wright historical sites has a dual purpose: to not only promote the name of Wright among the great architects but also get younger people interested in architecture through the popularity of the motion picture. Audiences will begin to see such historical sites as film locations, which will broaden their horizons, and perhaps they will read more about this legendary architect and the substantial legacy he left behind.

Marc Wanamaker,
Los Angeles and motion picture historian

INTRODUCTION

Friday night is movie night at our house. My wife, Ann; daughter, Elena; and I stream feature films on our big screen TV. One night in the fall of 2023 around Halloween, Elena (then twenty) picked the classic 1959 horror film *House on Haunted Hill*. I was surprised by her choice since she's rarely willing to sit through "old black and white movies." During the very first scene, where Vincent Price welcomes guests to his "haunted house" in the Hollywood Hills, I suddenly said, "Freeze it there!" I recognized one of Frank Lloyd Wright's buildings that I had included in my 2014 book *Frank Lloyd Wright on the West Coast*. It was the Ennis House, built in 1924, one of six homes Wright designed in the greater Los Angeles area. As we resumed watching the film, I thought to myself, "What a strange setting for a horror film," since it's very clearly an iconic example of Wright's modernistic residential designs with Mayan style overtones.

Over the next few days, I thumbed through my own book to check on how many Wright buildings in it had been used in feature films or TV series, which I had listed at the end of my descriptions of each building. It turned out there were seven such sites in California; five were in Southern California, and two were in Northern California. These included such popular films as *Blade Runner*, *Rush Hour*, *A Summer Place*, *The Rocketeer*, *Gattaca* and *Grand Canyon*, as well as some lesser-known films that have grown in popularity since their release, such as George Lucas's first feature film, *THX 1138*; *The Replacement Killers*; and *Permanent Midnight*. I've also included a sixth house in Los Angeles that a popular animated TV series used as a

Scene from *House on Haunted Hill* with guests' cars arriving to spend the night at Vincent Price's house.

setting for two characters and Joel Silver's film production company used as their logo.

So, I conceived the idea of a book about such iconic sites that would tell the story of how each production chose to use these sites, who was filmed in those scenes, and the history of the buildings themselves. I was aware of the fact that many of the Frank Lloyd Wright buildings that were used in films were in Illinois, Pennsylvania and New York City. But most Wright buildings used as locations for feature films were in California. After my initial contact with The History Press, their West Coast Acquisitions Editor Laurie Krill suggested focusing on the California sites, since that is the locus of the American film industry, and many of the tourists who come to the state every year are interested in seeing the locations where scenes from their favorite movies were filmed. The photographer I had worked with on my three previous books about historic architecture, Joel Puliatti, was happy to provide his images of each of the eight Wright sites, many of which have never been published before. And FYI, there will be no spoiler alerts in this book about the ending of any of the films described here.

However, there was one problem with this project. It would be a monumental task to find the dozens of archival film images I wanted to include in my book. So, I contacted Marc Wanamaker, a well-respected film historian and author who founded Bison Archives. He had provided several of the archival photos for my previous three books. Marc graciously offered to obtain all the film images you see in this book and was happy to write the foreword, since he's an expert on film locations.

Each of the Frank Lloyd Wright sites in this book has a separate chapter. Some of these sites have only had a single movie filmed there, such as the Pearce House, where several scenes in *Permanent Midnight* were filmed. Other sites have had multiple movies shot there, such as the Ennis House, which has been used in at least thirteen feature films to date. Every chapter includes a "box" of information with some of the most important facts about each of the films shot there: date of release, studio, director, main actors, running time, budget and box office receipts for major studio releases.

A note on sources for this book. A number of websites purport to list specific films that included scenes shot at Frank Lloyd Wright buildings, but some such websites include incorrect information. For example, the "FLW Sites" website has a page called "Movies Filmed in Wright Buildings" that lists the 1988 Bruce Willis film *Die Hard* as using the John Storer House for one of its locations. Yet there are no sites that remotely resemble a Wright building in this film! Also, Wikipedia's article on the Storer House states it's "prominently featured" in the film *The Rocketeer*. As it happens, it's the Ennis House that's featured in that film. Although the two houses have similar features, anyone familiar with Wright's Los Angeles buildings can tell the difference. The widely recognized authority on film locations is the IMDb website, which is why I used it for much of my research on which films were shot at specific Frank Lloyd Wright locations. Wikipedia also has detailed articles on these films, so I included some information from them, only when it was clearly sourced. One other website that has accurate information on films with Frank Lloyd Wright locations is called "Frank Lloyd Wright in Movies," which gives brief mentions of four Frank Lloyd Wright sites that were used in feature films and TV series.

A note about the use of the term *location*. The studios that produced some feature films included in this book chose to build a set of the interiors of Wright buildings that were settings for some scenes, either to control lighting conditions or avoid liability. When this is clearly established, I included that information here. Since IMDb still lists those films as having used a specific Wright building as a location, film historians agree that the use of such accurate reproductions of his sites, which set designers had to visit before creating these sets, makes it valid to describe them as Frank Lloyd Wright film locations. The focus of this book is primarily on feature films that used

Frank Lloyd Wright at his drafting table at Taliesin West, circa 1958. *Courtesy of Harold Stockstad Slide Collection, Anne T. Kent California Room, Marin County Free Library.*

Wright-designed buildings for one or more of their scenes. However, I've also included mentions or brief descriptions of some of the more popular TV series that have used Wright sites for one of their settings. They include *Twin Peaks*, *Buffy the Vampire Slayer*, *Westworld*, *Star Trek: Deep Space Nine* and *The Venture Bros*. The *Westworld* and *Star Trek: Deep Space Nine* series have longer descriptions, since they had direct tie-ins with previously filmed movies. Several music videos have also been filmed in Wright buildings, many of which are listed at the end of the chapters on those sites. I have also included an appendix with information about "How to Visit These Wright Buildings That Are Open to the Public."

I hope you enjoy reading this book as much as I enjoyed writing it. It combines two of my favorite topics, film history and Frank Lloyd Wright architecture. When I taught film history at Berkeley City College in the early to mid-2000s, my classes were always over-enrolled, and most of my students were eager to know where some of their favorite films were shot. And my experience of working as a freelance location scout for the 1983 film *The Right Stuff* gave me a much greater appreciation for the work film production companies do in choosing the best sites for each scene in the movies they create. So, I am happy to be able to add to the growing body of books about film locations so that students of film history, and you, can go to the locations of the movies included here, and then watch those films to recognize Frank Lloyd Wright's important place in America's cinematic legacy.

Mark Anthony Wilson,
Berkeley, California,
February 2025

1

FRANK LLOYD WRIGHT'S LEGACY IN THE HISTORY OF AMERICAN FILM

Frank Lloyd Wright's influence on the history of the American film industry has been considerable. Many of his most iconic buildings have been used as sites for scenes in some of Hollywood's most successful films. These range from *Blade Runner*, starring Harrison Ford; to *Rush Hour*, with Jackie Chan; to *Black Rain*, starring Michael Douglas; and *Gattaca*, starring Jude Law, Ethan Hawke, and Uma Thurman. As of this writing, there have been twenty feature-length movies that used Wright buildings just in California for one or more scenes and at least a dozen more that were partly filmed at Wright sites east of the Rocky Mountains, such as the Guggenheim Museum in New York City. In addition, at least five TV series and several music videos have used one of Frank Lloyd Wright's California buildings as locations. The criteria for movies included in this book is that they are American-made feature films distributed by a major studio with a theatrical release in several theaters.

Acclaimed director Ridley Scott, who directed both *Blade Runner* and *Black Rain*, stated why he chose to use Wright's Ennis House as a major location for the dark and dystopian world portrayed in *Blade Runner*, where most of the main scenes take place at night. In his vision of this future world, he was quoted as explaining that "Frank Lloyd Wright's architectural pattern strengthens the film's decadent and postmodern feel."

Wrought-iron gates at the main entrance to the Ennis House, where over a dozen feature-length movies have been filmed. *Photo by Joel Puliatti.*

Wright's influence on American films goes well beyond the film directors who chose his buildings for scenes in their movies. Two of Hollywood's most legendary creative geniuses, Walt Disney and Alfred Hitchcock, admired Wright's design philosophy of "organic architecture" and were influenced by his work in their own creative projects. Walt Disney maintained a personal friendship with Wright for many years and solicited his opinion on a number of design issues related to his films. One of Wright's most famous buildings was an influence for the design of one of the early installations at Disneyland.

Fans of Alfred Hitchcock films (and what serious film buff isn't?) may wonder what he and Frank Lloyd Wright could possibly have to do with each other. They were not friends and did not have any social interaction during their storied careers. And yet in Hitchcock's 1959 film *North by Northwest*, the final scene is set at a mid-century home that audiences have assumed for more than six decades was designed by Frank Lloyd Wright. In fact, to this day some visitors to nearby Mount Rushmore have asked to see this house. Whenever I would watch that film with family or friends, it seemed likely that house *was* designed by Frank Lloyd Wright.

When I was visiting friends in Paris in the 1990s, I talked with a French architectural historian who had written her doctoral thesis on Wright's

Usonian-style mid-century residential designs, and she had included the house at the end of *North by Northwest* as being a "classic example" of Wright's work in the 1950s. I wasn't sure if she was correct, so when I returned home, I did some research and found out that this house was actually never built! Hitchcock may have wanted Wright to design such a house for that film, but that never happened; therein lies an interesting story, which is told in my last chapter.

Another indication of Wright's influence on the American film industry is that there have been several films that included design details from one of Wright's buildings as part of a larger set that was not a reproduction of one of his sites. A good example of such borrowing of Wright motifs appears in the 1995 film *Mulholland Drive*, directed by David Lynch. Lynch had tile casts made of the decorative patterns Wright designed for the concrete blocks along the walls of the Charles Ennis House, which were then used to decorate the doorframe of the Club Silencio. The film *Beverly Hills Cop 2* also includes a Wright-inspired design motif along the entryway of the Beverly Hills Shooting Club, where Eddie Murphy goes to confront one of the criminals he's investigating. And in the 1990 film *Predator 2*, starring Danny Glover, one scene that takes place in a drug lord's apartment displays columns in the living room with vaguely Mayan-style motifs clearly inspired by those in the Ennis House, but they are clumsy and heavy-handed and not a copy of any of Wright's designs.

Besides those films that have used Frank Lloyd Wright buildings as locations, Wright's importance and reputation as America's most famous architect has found its way into the dialogue of other Hollywood movies. Some characters in feature films refer to Wright as part of their own identity or that of other characters. For instance, in the 2006 film *The Lake House* starring Keanu Reeves and Sandra Bullock, Reeves plays a young Chicago architect who moves into an all-glass house on a rural lakefront site. It was designed by his now deceased father, played by Christopher Plummer, who was a highly successful architect. Early in the film, we see Reeves talking to his father years before, and he then acknowledges his father's success by saying, "I know you played cards with Frank Lloyd Wright and Mies van der Rohe." Although it may be a stretch to imagine a building designed by Keanu Reeves, this scene is a testimony to how much of a cultural icon Frank Lloyd Wright had become by the early twenty-first century.

Another example of how Wright's architectural legacy affected Hollywood films was the making of the 1949 film *The Fountainhead*, based on the best-selling 1943 novel of the same title by controversial writer Ayn Rand. Rand also wrote the screenplay for this movie, which stars Gary Cooper, Raymond Massey and Patricia Neal in the main roles. It tells the story of Howard Roark, a "visionary architect" who fights to maintain "the integrity" of his modernistic buildings despite "pressures to conform to popular taste." The instructions Rand gave the set designers about how Roark's style should be portrayed stipulated, "It is the style of Frank Lloyd Wright—and *only* Frank Lloyd Wright—that must be taken as the model for Roark's buildings. This is extremely important to us, since we must make the audience admire Roark's buildings." However, the set designers Warner Bros. hired must not have studied Wright's work very closely, since none of Roark's designs in the film resemble Wright's buildings. Indeed, one critic described them as "horrible modernistic buildings" that were "embarrassingly bad." Unfortunately for the film's producers, Wright turned down an offer to help with designs for the buildings in this film. The one structure that *was* inspired by Wright's work appears at the end of the film, when Roark is seen standing on top of his "tallest building in the world." This evokes Wright's often stated desire to design the "world's tallest building" and his later preliminary plans for a mile-high skyscraper, a goal which modern high-rise projects seem to be aiming to achieve in the not-too-distant future.

Wright's work was also an inspiration for some film and series locations that were designed by architects who were clearly influenced by Wright's design philosophy. One such site is the Sheats-Goldstein House in Beverly Hills. It was completed in 1962 by John Lautner, who was an apprentice of Frank Lloyd Wright for many years. In the 1998 Coen brothers' film *The Big Lebowski*, Jeff Bridges' character "The Dude" settles into this house, which does not contain a single right angle and features a geometric grid-pattern on an overhanging ceiling in the living room, with picture glass windows that provide panoramic views of Los Angeles below. These are very "Wright-like" features, found on many of his "ship's prow" Usonian homes, such as the Walker House in Carmel.

Wright's influence continues to be felt in the settings for more recent film and TV series productions. In HBO's blockbuster series *Game of Thrones*, the Meereen palace of the Queen of Dragons, Daenerys Targaryen, was inspired by Wright's Mayan Revival houses in the Los Angeles area, such as the Ennis House. The Australian-born architect and set designer Deborah Riley, who designed the sets for several episodes of this series, explained how Wright's work inspired her. "These buildings have a certain domesticity to them, but they also felt sort of monolithic and ancient at the same time."

As of this writing, a new movie project has decided to use a Frank Lloyd Wright site as a location, evidence that Wright's buildings are still seen as ideal settings for feature films. This film is a psychological thriller called *DreamQuil*, starring Elizabeth Banks and John C. Riley. The director, Alex Prager, chose the Marin County Civic Center in San Rafael for some of its scenes. This film will add to the list of movies with dystopian themes that chose this iconic Wright site as a location because it evokes the feeling of a futuristic world for their audiences.

Wright lived in Los Angeles from 1923 until 1925, after moving there from Chicago with his second wife. Between 1917 and 1925, he designed five homes built of concrete for well-to-do clients. The first of these residences was the Aline Barnsdall House, which is now known as "Hollyhock House." Barnsdall was a supporter of performing arts companies, and through her, Wright met people involved in the entertainment industry in Southern California, which was beginning to blossom in those years. His commissions in the Los Angeles area helped him to develop a lifelong interest in the American film industry and in the movies it produced. Wright felt that his creative endeavors gave him something in common with the best Hollywood film makers, such as Alfred Hitchcock and Walt Disney.

Frank Lloyd Wright died at the age of ninety-one on April 9, 1959, before all but two of the movies that used his buildings had been released. If he had lived long enough to see some of those other films, he would undoubtedly have been pleased to witness how his work served as an inspiration to film directors and set designers. By choosing his buildings as locations, they were acknowledging how his creative genius had profoundly influenced their work. Wright loved screening feature films for the staff at his studio complex in Arizona, Taliesin West, from the late 1930s to late '50s, a period many film historians consider Hollywood's golden age. So, as you watch some of the films described in this book, they will give testimony to Frank Lloyd Wright's enduring place in the history of American film.

Frank Lloyd Wright in his San Francisco office, circa 1950s. *Courtesy of Anne T. Kent California Room, Marin County Free Library.*

A NOTE ON PRIVACY: Six of the buildings in this book are private residences that are not open to the public, and the two other sites both require appointments or reservations to enter, as noted in an appendix at the end of this book. Please respect the privacy of the homeowners and/or residents of these buildings, and don't intrude onto their property when viewing them from adjacent public thoroughfares.

2

VINCENT PRICE'S DECEPTIVE INVITATION AND HARRISON FORD'S RELUCTANT NARRATION

CHARLES ENNIS HOUSE, 2655 GLENDOWER AVENUE, LOS ANGELES

The Charles Ennis House was completed in 1924 and is one of Wright's "textile block" houses in a style that has come to be called "Mayan Temple" or "Mayan Revival." Crowning a steep hillside lot in the Los Feliz District of Los Angeles, this was Wright's largest residential design on the West Coast at ten thousand square feet. It also has the distinction of having been used as a location in more feature films than any other Wright-designed residence, at least thirteen between 1933 and 1999. The Los Feliz District has long been favored by movers and shakers in the film industry, including producers, directors and studio owners, which is one reason that it was chosen as a location for so many Hollywood movies. The original clients, Charles and his wife, Mabel, were owners of a popular men's clothing store. This massive, rambling concrete home dominates the crest of a cliff that overlooks the streets of Hollywood and the Los Angeles Basin far below (Hollywood is not a separate town, but a district within the LA city limits).

The impressive south façade of the Ennis House is composed of long rows of setbacks that culminate in a wide central tower. Seen from below, it gives the appearance of a low-lying Mayan pyramid perched atop a hill. This house is a prime example of Wright's fascination with Pre-Columbian architecture during the 1920s, when he designed five Mayan-inspired

South façade of the Ennis House in the Los Feliz district of the Hollywood Hills. *Photo by Joel Puliatti.*

residences in the Greater Los Angeles area. Yet as anyone knows who has visited such sites in Central America, Mayan pyramids were never perched atop steep hills. Thus, with this house, Wright made unique use of its natural setting. Besides the setback massing of the façade of the Ennis House, Wright also designed interlocking geometric bas-relief patterns along the upper walls and columns inside that resemble decorative motifs found on the walls of Mayan temples.

The textile block construction Wright used here was employed on three of his other Mayan Temple–style homes, (see chapters 5 and 6). This method essentially involved using two parallel rows of twelve-inch-thick square concrete blocks for the walls with an air pocket between them. Steel reinforcing rods were then inserted between the blocks at even intervals to tie the blocks together and stabilize the walls.

The front entrance to the Ennis House is along the north side along Glendower Avenue. Wright created a hidden private entrance behind an ornate, cast-iron grillwork gate, down a set of steps and beneath a long overhang projecting from the west side. The front door is to the left of a wide plaza that wraps around the west and south sides of the house. This plaza affords mesmerizing panoramic views of the LA Basin. A large outdoor pool

The main deck on the south side of the Ennis House, with a view of greater Los Angeles. *Photo by Joel Puliatti.*

was set into the plaza in 1940, which a subsequent owner had Wright design. Both of these features appear in several movies that were filmed here.

The interior of the Ennis House is quite impressive. There are two levels of living space. A spacious living room with high ceilings supported by two-story-tall textile block columns graces the main level. It has a tall leaded glass window facing south, which has a magnificent view of Hollywood and downtown Los Angeles. Wright designed a wisteria vine pattern for this window, one of his last uses of decorative art glass on any residence. There is a large fireplace on the north wall of the living room, beyond a loggia built of tall pillars made of patterned textile blocks. Running along the east wall of the living room is a deep balcony, which allows the owners to look out over their guests as they arrive. It was sometimes used as a "musicians perch" for entertaining during large social gatherings. At the east end of the house are two bedrooms and a bath, including the master bedroom. A half level up is the dining room, which faces south to catch the light and the best views.

The hallways in the Ennis House are long, gallery-like passageways lined with decorated textile block pillars. This creates the appearance of a temple or cathedral aisle, but because of Wright's use of tall, picture glass windows throughout most of the house, these hallways are much brighter than those in a temple or a church. He also used teakwood for the doors and window frames in each room, creating a pleasing textural and color contrast to the dominant beige color of the exposed textile block walls.

Wright designed the Ennis House in 1923, and the construction on it and the separate chauffeur's quarters was completed in 1924. Below the house is a twenty-foot-tall retaining wall also made of textile blocks to help stabilize the massive structure. Despite this wall, the house had serious structural problems even before construction was completed. Some of the concrete blocks cracked, and the lower section walls buckled from the load of the section above them. This problem was largely due to impurities in the crushed granite that was mixed to make the concrete, as well as air pollution, which by the 1920s was already bad in Los Angeles. Thus, a protective coating was applied to the walls in an attempt to solve this problem, which slowed down the decay of the textile blocks but didn't stop it. By the time the Northridge Earthquake of 1994 hit the greater Los Angeles area, many of the concrete blocks were failing badly, and the quake exacerbated the problem.

In 1981, the eighth owner of the Ennis House, August Brown, donated it to the Los Angeles nonprofit Trust for Preservation of Cultural Heritage (now called the Ennis House Foundation), which began raising funds for the

North façade of the Ennis House. *Photo by Joel Puliatti.*

restoration of the home. The house sat empty for several years while the group sought funds for this project, which they estimated would require $5 million for stabilizing the foundation and $15 million for the full restoration of the house itself. After a FEMA grant and private bank loan were obtained, the work began in 2006. The essential repairs were completed in 2007 at a cost of $6.4 million. The foundation put the house on the market in 2009, but the Great Recession made it difficult to find a buyer.

Finally, in July 2011, the house was sold to business executive Ron Burkle for just under $4.5 million. Burkle had experience with restoring and maintaining historic houses in the Los Angeles area, including silent film comedian Harold Lloyd's home. Burkle undertook the task of finishing the remaining repairs that the Ennis House Foundation had been unable to complete. As part of the terms of the sale, Burkle agreed to allow the public to have access to the house twelve times a year in an easement binding on subsequent owners. Burkle sold the house in 2019 for $18 million to Robert Rosenheck and Cindy Capobianco, cannabis industry entrepreneurs and philanthropists. The appendix will explain why, at the time of this writing, it is not feasible for people interested in seeing the Ennis House to arrange a visit.

Female (1933)

This was the first Hollywood feature film to include scenes shot at the Ennis House. It was a "pre-code" film and considered quite controversial when it was released. The Hays Code was a self-imposed set of moral standards for all Hollywood films released between 1934 and 1968. It prohibited depictions of anything that "lowers the moral standards of the viewing audience." Prohibited acts included profanity, graphic violence, actual or suggested nudity and "sexual persuasions." Although *Female* did not include any profanity or violence, it did include scenes with suggested nudity and sexual persuasions, even though those scenes are mild by today's standards. However, the main controversy the film created was its depiction of an independent woman named Alison Drake, the president of an automobile company, who controls the men around her and refuses to get married. Some of her comments about marriage and relationships with men were upsetting for many audiences at the time, which is one reason the film did not do very well at the box office.

The star of this film was Ruth Chatterton, a respected 1930s actress who was a leading lady in several other films with strong female characters. As

Scene from *Female*, with Ruth Chatterton and a male guest at her pool, one of her many would-be lovers.

the movie begins, she is visited by an old schoolmate who is married with three children and is surprised to hear that Alison has never married. Alison invites her friend to come with her to her house after work. In the next scene, we see Alison's chauffeur-driven limo pass through the front gate of the Ennis House. But when they go inside, the interior is a set with white walls and Streamline Moderne Art Deco décor, bearing no resemblance to the Mayan Temple style of Wright's design.

The two friends talk while Alison gets a massage wearing only a towel, and Alison then steps into a shower stall. When her friend asks her why she has never married, Alison replies, "I decided to travel the same open road as men travel. So, I treat men exactly the way they've always treated women." And when her friend asks if she doesn't regret not having a family and a husband, Alison explains, "You can't work with men fourteen hours a day and not lose your girlish illusions. I see lots of men, but I've never found a real one."

A few minutes later, we see the rear façade of the Ennis House as Alison and a man she invited from work sit by a large Art Deco–style pool

Ruth Chatterton, who played the main character in *Female*, standing at her pool in the "backyard" of the Ennis House, which was a set.

with a richly landscaped garden beyond it, complete with a tall fountain. Since none of these features exist on the grounds of Ennis House, this is clearly an elaborate set. After a few minutes of suggestive banter during which the male employee hopes Alison will let him stay for the night (as she has done with other men from her company), she becomes bored with him and tells him to leave. She has similar encounters with other men in a later scene, when she throws a pool party in the backyard of her house and fends off the attentions of several eager men, whom she is convinced are only after her money. Bored by all the "fake flattery" of the men at her party, she leaves, driving herself downtown to seek amusement, where she meets the "handsome" Jim Thorne, played by George Brent. The rest of this film shows the back-and-forth interactions between these two characters, which include some unexpected twists that are more creative than those in most modern rom-coms.

FILM FACTS

Directors: William Wellman, William Dieterle,
Michael Curtiz
Studio: First National Pictures
(distributed by Warner Bros.)
Release Date: November 11, 1933
Stars: Ruth Chatterton, George Brent, Lois Wilson
Running Time: 60 minutes
Budget: $286,000
Box Office Gross: $451,000 (estimated)

HOUSE ON HAUNTED HILL (1959)

This black-and-white horror film about an allegedly haunted house was only the second feature film to use the exterior of Ennis House as a location. It stars Vincent Price, Carol Ohmart and veteran character actor Elisha Cook (who played the hapless gunsel in *The Maltese Falcon*). The film starts with a black screen for several seconds as we hear bloodcurdling screams and the voices and laughter of ghosts. Then we see the face of Elisha Cook, the owner, describing the murderous history of the house, where seven people have been murdered "since it was built a century ago" (the Ennis House was only thirty-five years old at the time). Next, Vincent Price's face is shown superimposed over the north façade of the house, shown at an oblique angle from the right side. It's nighttime, and the house is unevenly lit, giving it a mysterious, ominous look. Price tells us that he's rented this house for one night and invited five people to a join his "haunted house party." He says they will each earn $10,000 "if they can survive the night!"

In the next scene, we see a line of cars driving up the steep slope of Glendower Avenue. There are five cars, one for each guest, and Price's voice describes each one as they are shown being driven by chauffeurs to the entrance. He explains the motivations of these guests are either a desperate need for money or greed. The cars drive through the cast-iron gateway and let the guests out on the plaza. One of the guests stands for a moment at the edge of the plaza, taking in the view of the city lights below. Then the guests approach the entrance, and the front door

DO YOU DARE ENTER?
HOUSE ON HAUNTED HILL
starring VINCENT PRICE
CAROL OHMART · RICHARD LONG · ALAN MARSHAL
Produced and Directed by WILLIAM CASTLE · Written by ROBB WHITE · AN ALLIED ARTISTS PICTURE

Opposite: Poster from *House on Haunted Hill* with Vincent Price and a skeleton, like one used as a gimmick in theaters that showed this film.

Top: Scene from *House on Haunted Hill*, with Vincent Price's face superimposed over the Ennis House, where he paid guests to spend the night if they could survive until dawn.

Bottom: Vincent Price inside his "haunted house." This interior was a set in an ersatz version of a Victorian-era living room, bearing no resemblance to the interior of the Ennis House.

slowly swings open to reveal—a totally different house that bears no resemblance to Wright's design for the interior! Instead, the guests enter a set the producers built to look like a Victorian mansion, a more familiar setting for a haunted house. The décor and furnishings of this set have a neo-Victorian kitsch ambience, decidedly less authentic than most other films about haunted houses.

The rest of the film consists of a series of over-the-top staged appearances by "ghosts" and "monsters" to frighten the guests into leaving before morning comes, which causes one young female guest to let loose with earsplitting screams several times before the movie ends. The famous "walking skeleton" incident in the final scene seems laughably corny now, but many audiences found it truly frightening at the time. The film's director/producer, William Castle, used life-size plastic models of this skeleton to promote the movie in theaters. The prop would float out from behind the screen on a wire above the audience before each showing, eliciting screams from many patrons. A colorized version of the film is available on various streaming services, but the original black-and-white look is more appropriate for the mood of the story. There was a remake of the film in 1999, but it has not achieved the same level of popularity as the original film. The 1959 film has become a cult classic, popular today with three generations of viewers, as my Gen Z daughter can attest. On the IMDb rating system for movies, *House on Haunted Hill* (1959) received a 6.7 out of 10 rating.

FILM FACTS

Director: William Castle
Studio: Allied Artists Pictures
Release Date: February 17, 1959
Stars: Vincent Price, Carl Ohmart,
Richard Long, Carolyn Craig, Elisha Cook
Running Time: 76 minutes
Budget: $200,000 (estimated)
Box Office Gross: $2.5 million

THE TERMINAL MAN (1974)

This was the first color film to use the Ennis House as a location. It's an early example of a dystopian science fiction movie, based on a 1972 novel of the same title by Michael Crichton. It was also one of the first American films to use the term *artificial intelligence* to refer to the concept of human-made devices that have the capacity to think independently of their creators. This film should appeal to conspiracy theorists who believe computer chips are being secretly implanted in our brains to control human behavior.

The central character is Harry Benson, a "brilliant computer scientist" with an IQ of 144, played by George Segal. Benson has an unusual form of epilepsy, which causes him to black out whenever he has a seizure and awake in a strange setting, believing that he committed acts of violence during these blackouts. The story begins as he gets sent to prison after one of these episodes, and he agrees to be a candidate for a new medical procedure that he hopes will cure him of this condition. The surgeon who is to perform this operation is Dr. John Ellis, played by Richard Dysart, the head of his own research lab in a major Los Angeles hospital. Ellis's plan is to implant a microcomputer in Benson's brain to control his seizures, thus suppressing his violent impulses by preventing his blackouts. However, his psychiatrist, Dr. Janet Ross played by Joan Hackett, is against this procedure. She worries that the experiment could backfire and make Benson psychotic due to his brain merging with the computer, thereby making him even more prone to violent episodes. She tells Dr. Ellis and his staff about these concerns, reminding them that Benson believes that "machines were competing with humans" for control of the world. They ignore her and proceed with the operation. The operation scene lasts nearly thirty minutes, and each step is shown in painstaking (some might say mind-numbing) detail.

The operation appears to be a success at first. Dr. Ross interviews Benson afterward at the hospital, asking him how he feels now. He says he feels fine and doesn't believe his violent seizures will return. But he does display heightened sexual desires toward her while they talk, portending a serious side effect of the experiment. Dr. Ross recommends he be given time to rest in his hospital room so he can fully recover from his operation.

In the meantime, Dr. Ellis hosts a party at his house to celebrate the "success" of his experiment. His home is the Ennis House. Fifty-six minutes into the film, he is shown walking down the long hallway at night talking with some guests about how well the procedure went and the possibilities for using his technique to "cure" other patients. Then he enters the living room, where

Scene from *The Terminal Man*, with Richard Dysart and his guests in the long hallway of the Ennis House.

many other guests are drinking and celebrating this medical "breakthrough." But he soon gets a call from the staff at the hospital telling him that Benson has escaped and they have no idea how—or where he is at the moment.

The remainder of the film depicts Benson as he wanders around the Los Angeles area while suffering from increasingly long, intense and frequent seizures that cause him to commit even more violent acts than he had before the operation. The last forty minutes of this film are definitely more interesting than the previous hospital scenes. But by this time, many of those who saw this film during its brief theatrical release had likely lost interest in the story, as the paltry box office sales would indicate. All in all, *The Terminal Man* is a strange and disjointed film, but it deserves credit for attempting to deal with serious themes of mental illness, compulsive violent behavior and the ineffective and often harmful effects of an institutional response to dealing with these societal problems.

Critical and industry response to this film was mixed. *The New York Times* critic Nora Sayre found the movie to be dull and slow, writing, "George Segal's resilience, humor, and versatility have redeemed quite a few bad scripts. But this role gives him little opportunity to act, other than making like a zombie and rolling his eyeballs back." Stanley Kubrick watched the film before the studio's decision not to release it in Britain, and he told an executive at Warner Bros., "I've already seen it, and it's terrific." Director

Terrence Malik wrote to the film's director, "I've just come from seeing *The Terminal Man*, and want you to know what a magnificent, overwhelming picture it is. —Your images make me understand what an image is, not a pretty picture but something that should pierce one through like an arrow and speak in a language all its own."

FILM FACTS

Director: Mike Hodges
Studio: Warner Bros.
Release Date: June 19, 1974
Stars: George Segal, Richard Dysart, Joan Hackett, Donald Moffat, Jill Clayburgh
Running Time: 104 minutes
Budget: (not documented)
Box Office Gross: $225,000 (United States and Canada)

THE DAY OF THE LOCUST (1975)

This disconcerting look at the inner workings of the film industry is set in Depression-era Hollywood. It was faithfully adapted from the popular novel with the same name by Nathanael West. It received critical acclaim when it was released but was a box-office flop. However, it has gained respect and a steadily growing audience since then because of its unflinching look at the negative effects of an obsession with fame and success that Hollywood encourages. All of the main characters are harmed or corrupted in some way by their desire to "make it" in the film industry, or by the effects of that industry on the people they live with. This was the first feature film to use both the actual exterior and interior of the Ennis House as a location.

The story begins with a group of financially struggling residents of Mediterranean-style courtyard apartments that one of the residents, Tod, played by William Atherton, dubs "Early Earthquake" when he sees damaged plaster on the wall of his unit from the Long Beach earthquake of 1933. Tod is immediately smitten with his lovely blonde neighbor Faye, played by Karen Black. She lives with her father, played by Burgess Meredith, who tries in vain to earn money by selling patent medicines. He used to have a successful vaudeville act and keeps hoping he'll revive his career one day. Faye wants to be a movie star, and Tod is a talented artist who gets a job as an entry-level scene illustrator at Paramount Studios but has aspirations to become the top talent in his field. Tod begins dating Faye, who plays hard-to-get with him, much to Tod's palpable frustration.

Later in the film we meet Homer Simpson (no relation to the cartoon character), a lonely bachelor played by Donald Sutherland, who soon falls desperately in love with Faye. He owns a comfortable house in a good neighborhood, so Faye moves in with him and takes cruel advantage of his trust and emotional dependence on her. Meanwhile, Tod shows his drawings one day to the studio set director, Claude Estee, played by Richard Dysart. Estee is impressed by Tod's talent and offers him the job of illustrating the scenes for one of the studio's major productions. They soon form a solid friendship, and Tod tries to forget about Faye while he concentrates on what looks to be a promising career. Meanwhile, Faye doesn't get any of the acting parts she auditions for and takes her frustrations out on hapless Homer.

About two-thirds of the way through the film, a disaster occurs on one of sets while Tod is on site; it suddenly collapses under the weight of the actors that are climbing on top of it during a battle scene. None of the actors are killed, but dozens of them are injured, some of them seriously. Estee tries to brush off the incident as inconsequential, but an investigation is required by the studio's insurance company. So, Estee invites Tod to his house to discuss

Scene from *The Day of the Locust*, with Richard Dysart walking down the long hallway of the Ennis House.

Scene from *The Day of the Locust* with Richard Dysart and William Atherton in the living room of the Ennis House.

how to get their "story straight" for the investigators so the studio can avoid any financial liability.

The house Estee lives in is the Ennis House, and it's seen in the mellow early evening light as Tod stands on the south plaza and gazes out at the entrancing view of the Hollywood Hills and Los Angeles. Estee walks down the long hallway to meet him. When he emerges to greet Tod, Estee says, "I think I fell in love with the house," a sentiment shared by the many owners who have actually lived there over the past century. While the two men chat on the deck, Tod notices there's a statue of a large white horse lying at the bottom of the pool. Estee explains to Tod, "Mrs. Estee thought we needed a horse in the swimming pool—so we got one!"

Tod and Estee then go inside and sit on the upper deck above the living room, with the two-story-tall columns visible beyond them. They discuss how to handle the insurance investigation, and Tod agrees not to say anything that would contradict Estee's cover story about the accident. They are next seen in front of the tall leaded glass window on the south wall of the living room, with its triple lights and wisteria vine pattern framing the view. At the end of this scene, Tod is shown standing up as he's framed by this window in a soft light. He hesitates for a moment before leaving, and the expression on his face indicates he regrets having sacrificed his integrity to be successful in Hollywood.

The final section of *Day of the Locust* includes one of the most disturbing depictions of mass hysteria ever filmed, from which the book and film take their title. The overall effect of this movie is to leave audiences with the feeling of having witnessed an unflattering and brutally honest view of how Hollywood's version of the American dream can turn into a nightmare for many people. It was nominated for two Oscars, Best Supporting Actor for Burgess Meredith and Best Cinematography, but didn't win either one. The film received a Rotten Tomatoes rating of 63 percent over the years, a better than average score, particularly for a movie that was a box office flop at the time it was released.

FILM FACTS

Director: John Schlesinger
Studio: Paramount Pictures
Release Date: May 7, 1975
Stars: Burgess Meredith, Karen Black,
Donald Sutherland, William Atherton, Richard Dysart
Running Time: 144 minutes
Budget: $5 million (estimated)
Box Office Gross: $17,793,000
(United States and Canada)

BLADE RUNNER (1982)

This is by far the most popular movie that has ever used a California Frank Lloyd Wright building as a location. Ironically, it was not a big box office success when it was released. Yet it has gained a growing audience of dedicated fans in the years since then. Part of the reason for its expanding audience is the continuing controversy over the six versions of the film that have different endings, besides the original U.S. theatrical cut. There has also been a lot of online chatter about Harrison Ford's narration of the U.S. theatrical cut and how his attitude while doing that narration affected the film. Here, we focus on the "Final Cut," since that is the version most people have seen on DVD or streaming services since it was released in 2007 and the only version over which Ridley Scott retained artistic control. The film was based on a 1968 novel by Philip K. Dick called *Do Androids Dream of Electric Sheep?*

Blade Runner is one of two Ridley Scott films in which he chose to use the Ennis House as a location (Scott may have influenced David Lynch's use of

Mayan Revival motifs in *Mulholland Drive*), the other one being *Black Rain*. His admiration for Wright's work is obvious, both in the creative way he has filmed scenes set in the Ennis House and in statements he has made about why he chose Wright's work as a location. He explained his choice of the Ennis House in *Blade Runner* as the main character's apartment by saying he felt Wright's design "strengthens the decadent and post-modern feel" he was aiming for in this film.

The movie is set in a futuristic-looking Los Angeles in the year 2019, as the opening scene tells us. It is a dark, bleak world, decaying around the edges despite the technological advances seen in the architecture and infrastructure. The streets are teeming with crowds seeking release from their grim lives through some of the high-tech entertainment options available to them, or food from street vendors. The all-powerful Tyrell Corporation creates realistic-looking humanoid androids called replicants as a labor force for space colonies. One group of four replicants, led by gratuitously violent Roy Batty (played by Rutger Hauer) have escaped and are hiding out on earth. In this unrelentingly dystopian world, a weary former Blade Runner named Rick Deckard (played by Harrison Ford) is grudgingly recruited by his former supervisor (played by Emmet Walsh) to hunt down and "retire" these replicants by terminating them. Blade Runners are a special force of policemen trained to hunt down and terminate renegade replicants.

When Deckard returns to his apartment thirty minutes into the film, we see the northern exterior of Ennis House as he drives through the entry gate, parks his car and walks up to the front door (the car seen

Scene from *Blade Runner*, with Harrison Ford in his apartment in the Ennis House, a set on a sound stage.

Harrison Ford in the kitchen of his apartment in *Blade Runner.*

here was in the original 1982 film and inspired Tesla's later Cybertruck model). When Deckard enters his apartment, it's a mostly accurate reproduction of some of the smaller rooms in Wright's 1924 design. The interior scenes of Deckard's apartment were shot on a set on a sound stage, which was done for several reasons. First, Ridley Scott wanted to create a look of decadence to symbolize the grim dystopian world Deckard lives in, and the actual rooms in Ennis House were not run down enough to create this effect. Second, the lighting conditions could be more easily controlled on a sound stage. Third, there would not be any liability issues if damage was caused by filming on a set.

All of the scenes inside Deckard's apartment have a dark, claustrophobic look, part of the reason why some online critics have described *Blade Runner* as creating a "futuristic film noir" feel. In the first apartment scene, a replicant named Rachael (played by Sean Young) is waiting for him. She doesn't know she's a replicant (though not one of the ones Deckard is hunting). When he tells her the truth and then goes into his rundown kitchen to get her a drink, she begins to cry and leaves. At the end of this scene, we see Deckard standing on a balcony, looking over a steep urban canyon below lined with futuristic skyscrapers. This is likely a composite image, since there are no balconies at the Ennis House that look straight down into an urban canyon, while the skyline was done with CGI.

An hour into the movie, Rachael reappears when she shoots dead another replicant on the streets of LA who's trying to kill Deckard. They go back to his apartment, where he washes out his wounds, and they end up making love. The last time we see Deckard's place is at the end of the film when he returns from a battle with Roy Batty to find Rachael in his bed, having fallen asleep waiting for him.

The controversy over Harrison Ford's narration of the theatrical cut was generated by his lackluster and uninspired tone of voice in each scene where he does voiceover. This task was forced on Ford by the film's producers because in advance screenings, test audiences had reacted poorly to the film, saying the narrative was confusing and incoherent, making it hard to understand what was going on. So, the producers decided using voiceover in key scenes would fix this problem, and they required a reluctant Ford to return to a studio to record the narration that the original theater audiences would hear. In the years since, reviews of Ford's voiceovers have ranged from "awful" to "terrible," though perhaps weary-sounding is a more appropriate description.

Even though it didn't achieve much success at the box office when it was released in 1982, *Blade Runner* did receive some acclaim from the film industry itself. It garnered two Academy Award nominations that year, for Best Art Direction and Best Visual Effects, but did not win an award in either category. Nonetheless, it holds an 89 percent rating on Rotten Tomatoes, one of the highest ratings ever for a science fiction movie.

FILM FACTS

Director: Ridley Scott
Studio: Warner Bros.
Theatrical Release Date: June 25, 1982
Stars: Harrison Ford, Rutger Hauer, Sean Young, Edward James Olmos, Daryl Hannah, M. Emmet Walsh
Running Time: 118 minutes (theatrical cut)
Budget: $28,000,000 (estimated)
Box Office Gross: $32,914,000 (United States); $41,762,000 (worldwide)

Karate Kid III (1989)

This is the third and final installment of the original Karate Kid series and the only one to use a Frank Lloyd Wright location. To say it was not as well-received by audiences or critics as the first two installments would be an understatement. The fight scenes and training sessions are over-the-top, and the dialogue is often ludicrous, with lines like, "Inside you same place you karate comes from," and "Mercy is for the weak—we do not train to be merciful here." Rotten Tomatoes gave this movie an audience score of 35 percent. But this film does have the distinction of doing a good job depicting what it would be like to live in a famous Frank Lloyd Wright house.

The plot revolves around the rivalry between the protagonist Daniel (played by Ralph Macchio) and a sadistic karate trainer named John Kreese (played by Martin Kove). They are both training to win a major karate tournament, Daniel as a contestant and Kreese as a trainer. Pat Morita reprises his role as Daniel's trainer Mr. Miyagi. Most of the online reviews agreed that one of the flaws in *Karate Kid III* is that it did not depict the relationship between Daniel and Miyagi as believably as in the first two films. In fact, noted *LA Times* critic Kevin Thomas characterized both the plot and characters' interactions as "a disaster of the most uninspired contrivances." Interestingly, the director, John Avildsen, also directed the *Rocky* film series.

The Ennis House first appears six minutes into the film, when we see the north façade shot from below between trees. Kreese is then seen walking along the hallway and entering the living room, where two kickboxers are training on the upper deck. One of them is Terry Silver (played by Thomas Ian Griffith), a corrupt businessman and the owner of the house. They greet each other and walk over to the large picture window with its view of downtown LA shrouded in smog. The two men plot to get "revenge" on Daniel and Miyagi for winning the last karate tournament against one of Kreese's students and causing Kreese to lose his karate studio. A few scenes later, the north exterior of Ennis House is shown at night, and next we see Silver inside on the phone in his home office, refining his plans for revenge. After finishing his call, he walks through the living room and out onto the deck to his car and leaves for an evening event. The third time the Ennis House is shown, we see Silver taking a bath as he greets his karate crew there. This scene was probably filmed on a set to control the lighting and avoid any water damage to one of the real bathrooms.

Scene from *Karate Kid III*, with karate fighters in the living room of the Ennis House. This film was nominated for five Golden Raspberry Awards.

Although *Karate Kid III* did not receive any of the traditional Hollywood awards for good films, it did achieve notoriety from one well-known film organization. It was nominated for five Golden Raspberry Awards: Worst Picture, Worst Actor (Ralph Macchio), Worst Supporting Actor (Pat Morita), Worst Director and Worst Screenplay. However, it did not "win" in any category.

FILM FACTS

Director: John Avildsen
Studio: Columbia Pictures
Release Date: June 30, 1989
Stars: Ralph Macchio, Pat Morita, Martin Kove, Thomas Ian Griffith
Running Time: 112 minutes
Budget: $12.5 million
Box Office Gross: $38,956,000 (worldwide)

BLACK RAIN (1989)

This international thriller was the second Ridley Scott film to use the Ennis House as a location. This time, Scott used the actual interiors for the setting of a key scene instead of a set, as well as the exterior. His cinematography in that scene makes much more imaginative use of the Ennis House than most other films have. Scott also was the first director to employ the Ennis House as the residence of an important Asian character, which other directors did in later films. *Black Rain* was a major box office hit, but it did not receive much critical praise except for its creative use of locations and sound effects. Most of the film was shot in Osaka, Japan, where the majority of the story takes place.

The plot of *Black Rain* is focused on New York City detective Nick Conklin, played by Michael Douglas. As the film opens, Conklin is being investigated by Internal Affairs for alleged corruption. The next day, Nick and his partner Charlie Vincent, played by Andy Garcia, witness a brutal hit in a bar when a Japanese yakuza gangster named Sato, played by Yûsaku Matsuda, bursts in and kills several Japanese men meeting with a mafioso. Then he steals a package from them. Nick and Charlie chase Sato down and arrest him. They are given the task of escorting him to Osaka after Japan asks for him to be extradited to face criminal charges there. When they land, Sato manages to give them the slip before the Japanese police arrive. Now they have to work with an English-speaking Osaka police detective named Matsumoto, played by Ken Takakura, to track down Sato and bring him to justice. The rest of the film focuses on the rivalry between Sato and a traditional yakuza boss named Kunio Sugai and the culture clash between two brash and impatient New York City detectives and the careful, more measured methods of Matsumoto.

About halfway through the film, Nick visits a nightclub hostess named Joyce, played by Kate Capshaw, at her apartment after he and Charlie had been attacked by Sato and his gang. The Mayan geometric-patterned tiles along the wall of her studio flat indicate that this is one of the smaller spaces in the Ennis House, which here is supposed to be in an older apartment building in Osaka, Japan.

Several scenes later, Scott shows us the home of powerful yakuza boss Sugai, played by Tomisaburô Wakayama. First we see the south façade of Ennis House dramatically lit with a bluish hue through raindrops, and the camera angle is from below and to the left, emphasizing the mass of the house. Next Scott shows us the living room, or great hall, with its two-story

Michael Douglas sitting on the deck in the living room at the Ennis House in *Black Rain*.

tall columns. Nick is now seated on the upper deck overlooking the living room, with his back to the spacious hall below. Sugai is seen facing him in front of the fireplace with flames from a roaring fire behind him. As he talks to Nick about how to deal with Sato, the entire room is bathed in a warm, orange light, which creates an eerie effect. Sugai explains to Nick what "black rain" means. His family had lived through the aftermath of the atomic bomb drop on Hiroshima, after which the rain that fell on the city was black from the dust and cinders hovering in the air.

The criticism that *Black Rain* got when the film was released was mainly about having a "cliché-driven" plot and its supposed cultural insensitivity. Critics and audiences in Japan were reported to have liked the film, however. In any case, it was nominated for Academy Awards in two categories: Best Sound and Best Sound Effects, though it didn't win either one. It received a 54 percent rating on Rotten Tomatoes.

FILM FACTS

Director: Ridley Scott
Studio: Paramount Pictures
Release date: September 22, 1989
Stars: Michael Douglas, Andy Garcia, Kate Capshaw, Ken Takakura, Yûsaku Matsuda, Tomisaburô Wakayama
Running Time: 125 minutes
Budget: $30,000,000
Box Office Gross: $134,200,000

THE ROCKETEER (1991)

This family-friendly adventure film was one of Disney Studio's best live action films of the 1990s, yet it has enough colorful characters and plot twists to keep the interest of adult viewers. Although it had disappointing box office earnings, it has garnered a steadily growing audience on streaming services. Viewers' reactions were mostly positive at the time of its release, and it now has an audience score of 67 percent on Rotten Tomatoes. It's also noteworthy as one of then-twenty-year-old Jennifer Connelly's first starring roles as an adult leading lady.

The story takes place in Los Angeles in 1938, on the eve of the outbreak of World War II in Europe. A young daredevil pilot named Clifford Secord, played by Billy Campbell, finds a rocket backpack misplaced by thieves. With the help of his scientist friend "Peevy" Peabody, played by Alan Arkin, they make some adjustments to it that allow Clifford to fly and control his speed and direction. Meanwhile, a swashbuckling actor named Neville Sinclair, patterned after Errol Flynn and played by Timothy Dalton, has hired a criminal gang to obtain this jetpack and bring it to him. We soon find out that Sinclair is an undercover Nazi spy, who wants to send the jetpack to Germany so it can be used to create an army of "flying supermen" to help win the coming war for the Third Reich. On the set of Sinclair's latest movie, we meet an aspiring actress named Jenny Blake, played by Jennifer Connelly, who is Clifford's erstwhile girlfriend. Howard Hughes, played by Terry O'Quinn, was the inventor of the rocket pack, and he enlists the FBI to retrieve it before Sinclair gets his hands on it. One of the assets of *The*

Timothy Dalton in the Ennis House living room with two-story columns in *The Rocketeer.*

Timothy Dalton and Paul Sorvino in the living room of the Ennis House in *The Rocketeer.*

Rocketeer is that it does a superb job of re-creating the setting and atmosphere of 1930s Los Angeles, from the fashions and the hairstyles to the cars and the aircraft, the architecture, the signage and the music.

Fifteen minutes into the film, the criminal gang hired by Sinclair, whose leader is played by Paul Sorvino, meets the actor in the grand living room of his house in the Hollywood Hills. This scene was filmed in the main hall of the Ennis House, and as the men discuss how to steal the jetpack, we see close-ups of the leaded glass windows, the fireplace and the Mayan motifs on the textile block columns. About an hour later, Jenny is kidnapped by Sinclair after he renders her unconscious and is taken to his house, where he intends to force her to get Clifford to turn over the jetpack to him. We see her awakening in a small upstairs bedroom at night and then talking to Sinclair in an adjoining bathroom as she pretends to go along with his demands. This scene was reportedly filmed on a set to control the lighting and avoid the possibility of damage to the actual house when Jenny tries to escape and is chased by Sinclair. The climatic scene was filmed at Griffith Observatory, located in the Hollywood Hills just below Ennis House, where group tours of nearby film locations gather to meet their tour guides and board the buses.

Although *The Rocketeer* received mixed reviews from film critics, it was nominated for a Hugo Award for Best Dramatic Presentation but lost out to *Terminator 2*. It also inspired a spinoff TV series on Disney Junior Channel in 2019 that got positive reviews from children's show critics but was canceled after a single season.

FILM FACTS

Director: Joe Johnston
Studio: Disney Pictures
Release Date: June 21, 1991
Stars: Billy Campbell, Jennifer Connelly, Alan Arkin, Timothy Dalton, Paul Sorvino, Terry O'Quinn
Running Time: 108 minutes
Budget: $35 to $40 million (estimated)
Box Office Gross: $46.7 million

GRAND CANYON (1991)

This social commentary film is patchwork of loosely related stories about a group of Los Angelinos from various walks of life who try to bridge the racial and economic canyons of life in a big American city in the 1990s. Although it was not a box office hit, the film did garner praise from most movie critics and earned a 79 percent rating on Rotten Tomatoes. The screenwriters, Meg and Lawrence Kasdan, were addressing the important issue of the racial divide that had been simmering just beneath the surface in the "palm tree ghettoes" of Southern California, a view that was validated four months after the film's release when these tensions exploded in the Rodney King police beating riots, which took at least 63 lives and injured more than 2,300 people.

The ensemble cast included some of the most popular Hollywood personalities of the 1990s: Danny Glover as Simon, a tow truck driver; Steve Martin as Davis, a producer of violent movies; Kevin Kline as Mack, a property manager; Mary McDonell as Mack's wife, Claire; Alfre Woodard as Jane; and Mary Louise Parker as Dee. The film begins as Mack drives home from a basketball game and his car breaks down in a dangerous neighborhood at night, where a gang surrounds his car and tries to steal it while he waits for a tow truck. Simon arrives just in time to talk the gang out of harming Mack and then tows his car to a lot, where the two sit and talk about how "crazy and fragile" life has become in LA. The next day, Davis gets shot in the leg by a thief who steals his watch. He recovers slowly in the hospital but will have a limp for the rest of his life. Meanwhile, Claire finds an abandoned baby she decides to adopt, and Mack is having an affair with his young assistant, Dee. Up to this point, *Grand Canyon* paints a pessimistic picture of life in late twentieth-century America, complete with the heavy-handed metaphor of police helicopters buzzing overhead in nearly every scene to symbolize the breakdown of society. But events take a turn for the better after Mack decides to help Simon's sister and nephew move to a safer community and then arranges for Jane to meet Simon for a date, which leads to a romance.

The Ennis House appears about seventy-eight minutes into the film, when Davis is shown having a mental therapy session in Claire's office. This scene takes place in a small sitting room on the main level of Ennis House, and the Mayan geometric patterns on the textile block walls are shown in close-up behind Davis as he sits and tells Claire about his decision to "stop making violent movies" after his near-death experience and focus on making films that "affirm the life force." But a few scenes later, he reverts to his old ways, telling Mack that "violence sells these days" and his films merely reflect the reality of modern urban life. Then Davis says one of the most original lines in the film, when he tells Mack, "All life's riddles are answered in the movies."

Critics generally gave the movie positive reviews. Rita Kempley of the *Washington Post* wrote, "Kasdan validates our fears, but he doesn't strip us of all hope, for the central image also promises something greater than ourselves." And Owen Glieberman of *Entertainment Weekly* wrote, "It's the sort of movie that says 'Life is worth living'. After a couple of hours spent with characters this enjoyable, the message—in all its sentimentality—

Steve Martin in a meeting room of the Ennis House during a therapy session in *Grand Canyon*.

feels earned." The movie was nominated for an Academy Award for Best Screen Play Written Directly for the Screen for Meg and Lawrence Kasdan but did not win.

FILM FACTS

Director: Lawrence Kasdan
Studio: 20th Century Fox
Release Date: December 25, 1991
Stars: Danny Glover, Steve Martin, Kevin Kline, Mary Louise Parker, Alfre Woodard, Mary McDonell
Running Time: 134 minutes
Budget: not recorded
Box Office Gross: $33,243,000 (United States); $40.9 million (worldwide)

THE GLIMMER MAN (1996)

This "police buddy picture" stars two of the most ubiquitous B movie actors of the 1990s: Steven Seagal and Keenen Ivory Wayans. The film was a flop at the box office and got only an 11 percent rating on Rotten Tomatoes, one of the worst ratings of any big budget buddy/cop movies. Critics lambasted the movie, with a typical comment coming from Leonard Maltin, who called it a "tired buddy/cop picture, even by Seagal's low standards." Its only original idea was to shoot most of the scenes during LA's brief rainy season. However, for diehard fans of Steven Seagal's violent action screen persona, the movie was not a disappointment.

Seagal plays Jack Cole, a former CIA agent now working as a homicide detective with the Los Angeles Police Department. He earned the name "Glimmer Man" because when he stalked his CIA targets, they would only see a "glimmer" of him before he killed them. His partner is Jim Campbell, played by Wayans, who doesn't like Cole's New Age methods. They team up to catch a brutal serial killer called the "Family Man" who is terrorizing the Greater LA Area. In one of the first scenes, a high school teacher threatens to kill himself by jumping out a window, but Detective Cole saves his life by tackling him to the floor. This heroic act leads the teacher's father, a powerful crime boss named Frank Deverell, to ask Cole to work for him as part of his personal security detail, but Cole turns him down, thus making an enemy out of Deverell. The rest of the movie consists of a series of convoluted and implausible confrontations between

Top: The crime boss in *Glimmer Man* at the large leaded window in the Ennis House, showing a rare rainy day in Los Angeles.

Bottom: Scene from *Glimmer Man* with Bob Gunton as a crime boss in his office in the Ennis House.

the main characters as Cole and Campbell seek the real identity of the Family Man and Deverell's role in the murders.

The Ennis House was used in three scenes in *Glimmer Man*. Thirteen minutes in, Deverell is shown having lunch with a partner in the upper-level dining room, which overlooks the living room. Next, they walk over to the large latticed window, with its view of the Hollywood Hills obscured by falling rain. About fifty-five minutes into the film, we see Deverell in the living room of Ennis House at night, conspiring with Cole's corrupt supervisor. The Mayan columns are lit by an orange glow. After the two men talk, Deverell goes out onto the deck, admires the view (without any rainfall this time) and jumps into the pool for a swim. In the third scene, about fifteen minutes later, Deverell is sitting in his home office watching TV, while his partner is in another small room on the phone with Wayans. The first scene was clearly shot at Ennis House, while the last two scenes may have used sets.

Film Facts

Director: John Gray
Studio: Warner Bros.
Release Date: October 4, 1996
Stars: Steven Seagal, Keenen Ivory Wayans, Brian Cox, Michelle Johnson, Bob Gunton
Running Time: 92 minutes
Budget: $45,000,000
Box Office Gross: $20,351,000 (U.S. and Canada); $45,000,000 (estimate, worldwide)

The Replacement Killers (1998)

This underrated crime thriller was famed Hong Kong action star Chow Yun-Fat's U.S. film debut. It also features Mira Sorvino in an unusual role as a forger of documents who teams up with Chow to fight a gang of assassins, quite a change from her first starring role as a prostitute with a heart of gold in the 1995 film *Mighty Aphrodite*. Although she didn't win any awards for her role in *Replacement Killers*, Sorvino's portrayal of a tough, no-nonsense woman who knows how to use a gun made her seem like a perfect match as Chow Yun-Fat's partner. The film did not do well at the box office and had mixed reviews from critics at the time of its release, but it has gained a growing audience of fans on streaming services in recent years.

The first use of the Ennis House is eleven minutes into the film, when Chinese triad crime boss Terence Wei, played by Kenneth Tsang, hires professional assassin John Lee, played by Chow, for revenge on a LAPD detective. Lee goes to meet Wei at his home, walks through the ornate front gate and enters the living room, where Wei is sitting at a table backlit by the large wisteria-pattern leaded window. Wei gives Lee his assignment, but when Lee arrives at the detective's home, he decides he can't carry out the hit since it's on the detective's seven-year-old son, who is playing with his father in the driveway. Lee's failure to follow orders makes him a target of Wei's wrath, who sends teams of hit men to kill his former assassin. Lee decides to flee to Hong Kong but doesn't have a valid passport, so he hires forger Meg Coburn, played by Sorvino, to create a fake one in her high-tech, one-woman shop. But before she can complete the job, a group of hit men burst into her shop and end up shooting it out with Lee and Meg, who now must stay close to Lee for her own safety.

The Ennis House also appears briefly in a second scene where Wei's henchmen walk down the long main hallway to tell him of Lee's "betrayal." This use of the Ennis House as the residence of a powerful Asian character is indicative of the director's view of it as having an Asian ambience, as was the case with Ridley Scott's use of it in *Black Rain*. Among the positive reviews of *The Replacement Killers* was the one by famed *Chicago Sun Times* movie critic Roger Ebert, who said that it

Scene from *The Replacement Killers*, with assassins at the Ennis House gates.

The crime boss in *The Replacement Killers* at his dining room table in the Ennis House.

was "as abstract as a jazz instrumental, and as cool and self-assured" and that the film created a "high gloss version of a Hong Kong action picture, made in America but observing the exuberance of a genre where surfaces are everything." However, the film received a rating of only 37 percent on Rotten Tomatoes.

Film Facts

Director: Antoine Fuqua
Studio: Columbia Pictures
Release Date: February 6, 1998
Stars: Chow Yun-Fat, Mira Sorvino, Michael Rooker, Kenneth Tsang, Jürgen Prochnow
Running Time: 87 minutes
Budget: $30 million
Box Office Gross: $19.2 million (United States); $39.5 million (worldwide)

RUSH HOUR (1998)

This buddy/cop film is one of the most entertaining ones of that genre and is a lot of fun to watch. The dialogue and repartee between the two main characters, played by Jackie Chan and Chris Tucker, is both clever and amusing. The inevitable culture clash between an Asian detective from Hong Kong and a Black LA cop is handled in a way that doesn't stereotype either one, and the chemistry between the two lead actors makes it obvious that they enjoyed working with each other. *Rush Hour* was a major box office hit and spawned two sequels, with *Rush Hour 4* in production as of this writing.

Jackie Chan plays Inspector Lee, a martial arts master with the Royal Hong Kong Police. The film opens in Hong Kong on the eve of the handover of the former British colony to China. The first scene depicts Lee trying to arrest a mysterious crime lord, Juntao, who's been stealing Chinese cultural treasures. He doesn't catch Juntao but retrieves the stolen objects. The next scene takes place in the dining room of the Ennis House, which here serves as the residence of the departing Chinese Consul Han, who is about to take up his new assignment in Los Angeles. At this farewell dinner, we also meet Lee's supervisor Thomas Griffin, played by Tom Wilkinson. About two minutes into this scene, Lee enters the dining room and tells Han he is presenting the recovered treasures to him as a going away present. While the men talk, a nighttime view of the Hong

Scene from *Rush Hour* with Tom Wilkinson in front of the large window in the Ennis House dining room. This was a set, while the view of Hong Kong was a cycloramic painting with electronic elements.

Jackie Chan in *Rush Hour*, in the same set with Tzi Ma.

Kong skyline is seen outside the large picture window. This view was likely created with a cycloramic painting with electronic elements, and given how smoothly the camera pans from the window to the dining room itself, the entire scene was probably filmed on a sound set. *Rush Hour* was the third feature film to use the Ennis House as the residence of an important Asian character.

The next scene was shot at the John Snowden House by Lloyd Wright, Frank's son, as Lee is shown walking through the living room. He stops to speak with Han's ten-year-old daughter, Soo Young, to whom he has been giving martial arts lessons. She tells him she will miss him after she and her dad move to Los Angeles, and it's evident from their conversation that she looks up to Lee as if he were her uncle. A few weeks after Han and Soo Young move to LA, she is kidnapped by one of Juntao's thugs. Han calls Lee in Hong Kong to come to LA to rescue her, since he doesn't trust the local police or FBI to get her back safely. But when Lee arrives at LAX, he is greeted by LAPD Detective James Carter, played by Chris Tucker, who has been chosen by his supervisor to "babysit" Lee at the request of the FBI, so they can work on the case without interference from a foreign detective.

The bulk of the film from that point on is focused on the humorous misunderstandings and conflicts created by the cultural differences between Lee and Carter as they pursue leads and fight with groups of bad guys in their search to catch the criminals who've kidnapped Soo Young and rescue her. Thomas Griffin turns up in LA as well, and the mystery surrounding the theft of Chinese cultural treasures and the kidnapping is revealed as the story unfolds. Jackie Chan has plenty of scenes that showcase his martial arts skills and incredible athleticism, and Chris Tucker's brash persona and outlandish comments provide constant amusement.

One of the features of *Rush Hour* that won praise from film critics as well audiences was the fact that Jackie Chan did all his own action sequences without stunt doubles. Roger Ebert's review praised Chan for doing this, as well as Chris Tucker for his comedic sense. Joe Leydon of *Variety* called the film a "formulaic but raucously entertaining action comedy." But Chan was reportedly unhappy with the action scenes because he felt they were too brief, unlike his Hong Kong movies, in which he is shown for ten minutes or so of uninterrupted combat for each fight sequence. Clearly, the producers felt that was too long for American audiences who were not familiar with Chan's Hong Kong action films. Yet the fact that Chan agreed to star in three sequels indicates that he must have enjoyed playing the character of Inspector Lee, despite not getting as much screen time as he did in his previous films.

One other indication of the cultural influence of *Rush Hour* is the fact that the Rotten Tomatoes audience review system was inspired by the film. Senh Duong, a major fan of Jackie Chan's Hong Kong films, wanted to track audiences' reaction to Chan's first major starring role in an American movie. So, he created the Rotten Tomatoes website in two weeks and launched it just before the release of *Rush Hour*. This movie achieved a 62 percent rating on Rotten Tomatoes, a respectable score for a buddy/cop film.

Film Facts

Director: Brett Ratner
Studio: New Line Cinema
Release Date: September 18, 1998
Stars: Jackie Chan, Chris Tucker, Tom Wilkinson, Elizabeth Peña, Chris Penn
Running Time: 98 minutes
Budget: $35 million
Box Office Gross: $244.4 million (worldwide)

THE THIRTEENTH FLOOR (1999)

This little-known science fiction thriller was ahead of its time in more ways than one. Its use of virtual reality technology was hardly a first, but its all-consuming effect on those who use it was predictive of the ever more advanced forms of virtual reality devices that were to be introduced in the coming years. And this film's theme of creating artificial beings that would develop minds of their own and begin to dominate the humans who've created them was a foreshadowing of the current controversy over the dangers that uncontrolled use of AI could unleash on the human race. *The Thirteenth Floor* was loosely based on a 1964 novel by Daniel F. Galouye called *Simulacron-3*.

The story is set in Los Angeles in 1999, where a group of scientists on the thirteenth floor of an LA high rise have developed a system to create a highly advanced version of virtual reality, one so real that those who engage with it actually feel like they have entered into this artificial world and can interact fully with any of its inhabitants. Even more problematic is the fact that the "people" in this virtual world develop their own consciousness and don't realize they are only computer-generated images. The virtual "reality" these scientists have created to test their invention and see if it's commercially viable is downtown Los Angeles in 1937. The film does a good job of creating an authentic 1930s setting and ambience.

The main characters are Hannon Fuller, played by Armin Mueller-Stahl, who owns the corporation that creates this virtual reality system; his

Scene from *The Thirteenth Floor*, with Craig Bierko in his apartment in the Ennis House.

daughter Jane Fuller, played by Gretchen Mol; Douglas Hall, played by Craig Bierko, who is Hannon's protégé and heir to the company; and Jason Whitney, played by Vincent D'Onofrio, a scientist who constantly pushes to have the VR device marketed so they can become rich. During one of his visits to the VR Los Angeles, Hannon is murdered, though it's not clear to the viewer at first if it was by one of the artificial inhabitants of 1930s LA or by someone in the real world after he returns from his journey. In any case, Hall becomes the lead suspect, and most of the rest of the story follows the back-and-forth between Hall and LAPD Detective Larry McBain, played by Dennis Haysbert, as Hall tries to prove his innocence. He interacts with Jane Fuller when she arrives in LA after hearing about her father's death. She explains to Hall the shocking truth about her father's work in creating virtual worlds set in different time periods. The film has several unexpected plot twists and a truly clever surprise ending. However, the script does become more convoluted as the story progresses, causing some reviewers to call it confusing.

The Ennis House appears in three scenes in *The Thirteenth Floor*, since it was used as Douglas's apartment. Eight minutes in, we see Douglass asleep in a bedroom at night. Then he gets up and walks along the hallway to the bathroom, where he sees a white shirt stained with Hannon's blood. The second time, about twenty-one minutes into the film, Douglas is shown at home again listening to his voice mail messages, including one from Hannon the night he died. The third time, about twenty-four minutes later, the LA police are shown running down the main hallway of Ennis House on their way to Douglas's bedroom to arrest him for murder.

FILM FACTS

Director: Josef Rusnak
Studio: Columbia Pictures
Release Date: May 5, 1999
Stars: Craig Bierko, Gretchen Mol, Armin Mueller-Stahl, Vincent D'Onofrio, Dennis Haysbert
Running Time: 100 minutes
Budget: $16 million
Box Office Gross: $18.5 million

This film did not do well at the box office, barely making more than its budget. It also did not receive much positive response from audiences or critics, getting a 30 percent rating from Rotten Tomatoes. Leonard Maltin's review was one of the more upbeat ones, writing, "Well-produced sci-fi in film noir style is interesting throughout, but too talky." The only award *The Thirteenth Floor* was nominated for was a Saturn Award for Best Science Fiction Film, but it lost to *The Matrix*.

TV Series and Music Videos

The Ennis House has appeared in a number of popular TV series over the past three decades. In the late 1990s to early 2000s show *Buffy the Vampire Slayer*, the exterior of the house is shown as the residence of the characters Angel, Spike and Drusilla. Interiors of the Ennis House were also used in several episodes of David Lynch's quirky early 1990s TV series *Northern Exposure*. Re-creations of parts of Ennis House were used as a set for several episodes of *Star Trek: The Next Generation*.

Several pop music videos were partially filmed at Ennis House. The R & B group 3T filmed the black-and-white 1996 music video "Why?" at Ennis House, which features Michael Jackson singing with the group in the living room. The video starts with a young woman in a bathing suit seen standing at the edge of the deck along the south exterior and then plunging into the pool and swimming to the opposite side. The group S Club 7 filmed their 2001 video "Have You Ever" with extensive use of both the exterior and interior in scenes showing them living in the house. Ricky Martin's music video for his 1998 song "Vuelve" also used the interior of Ennis House.

In addition to the thirteen feature films by major studios that used the Ennis House as a location, there were several minor films that are listed by IMDb as having had scenes filmed at Ennis House. These are movies that either were foreign made; went straight to home video, DVD or streaming; or did not have a multiple theater release.

3

BEN STILLER'S TOTAL MELTDOWN

THE WILBUR PEARCE HOUSE, 5 BRADBURY HILLS ROAD, BRADBURY

In the 1998 Hollywood movie *Permanent Midnight*, starring Ben Stiller and Elizabeth Hurley, Hurley's character lives in an elegant modern house in the suburban hills above Los Angeles with spectacular views of the city lights far below. It is the Wilbur C. Pearce House in the tiny affluent hillside town of Bradbury. Konrad Pearce, grandson of the original owners, began a restoration process in the early 2010s after years of deferred maintenance, with the goal of returning the home to the way it looked when it was completed in 1955.

Wilbur Pearce was a marketing executive with the Firestone Tire and Rubber Company, and his wife, Elizabeth, was an abstract artist and president of the Women's Art League in Akron, Ohio, before the couple moved to California. The Pearces met Frank Lloyd Wright when he gave a lecture in Akron about a proposed art museum. Wright agreed to design a house for them after they relocated to California. In 1950, the couple bought a two-acre lot along the eastern foothills of unincorporated Los Angeles County, with views of the Los Angeles Basin to the south and the San Gabriel Mountains and Angeles National Forest to the north. Wright drew up plans that same year for a single-story, two-plus bedroom, two-bath, 1,900-square-foot house. Once the Pearces saved enough money, construction began in 1954. Wright's original bid called for a budget of $15,000, but like many of his other residential designs, the final cost was much more, coming to double that figure.

The Pearce House is a variation of Wright's Usonian style, which was an attempt to create a system of supposedly affordable detached housing for middle-class families. These houses were all designed on a variant of a grid pattern, usually employing square modules for the floor plans and incorporating a number of Wright's signature features, such as concrete slab floors and carports (which Wright is credited with inventing). The Pearce House is a bit different than most Usonian houses; here, Wright used a pattern of segmented circles to draw up the floorplan and the exterior of the home. The materials Wright used on the Pearce House were concrete blocks for the walls, plate glass for the doors and windows, Douglas fir for the ceilings and Honduran mahogany overlay for the window framing. The floors are composed of concrete slabs in three-foot-square patterns stained "Cherokee red," one of Wright's favorite colors for Usonian houses.

By far the most distinctive feature of the Pearce House is Wright's use of a sweeping concave curve along the south façade. The north façade has a slightly convex curve along the west section of it. All the overhanging eaves are several inches wide, creating a strong visual line that extends around the entire perimeter of this flat-roofed house. These eaves partially shade the two terraces. The larger terrace, on the south side, runs nearly the entire length of the house, following the curve of the façade. There is a small pool set into this terrace. Konrad Pearce told me that while he was restoring the house, a family of black bears, a mother and her three cubs, would come down from Angeles National Forest at dusk several times a week and play in this pool (undoubtedly not the use Wright intended for it). Konrad also told me that his grandparents said the flat roof did not leak during rainy weather for the first ten years they lived there, which was a perennial problem with many of Wright's other flat-roofed houses, some of which developed roof leaks within a year or two after the owners moved in.

The main entrance to the Pearce House is on the northeast end. The plate glass front door opens directly into the living room, which is a wide-open space that doubles as the dining room with an adjacent open kitchen. This is an early use by Wright of the "open concept" floor plan, a feature that has become popular with millennial home buyers over the past decade or so (as anyone who has watched episodes of HGTV's *House Hunters* series will know). Wright placed a wall of floor-to-ceiling windows on both the south and north sides of this room. A glass door opens from the southeast corner of this room out onto the curved terrace, with another glass door opening onto the north terrace. Elizabeth asked Wright to alter his original design for the windows on the north side to allow for a full view of the nearby mountains.

South façade of the Pearce House. *Photo by Joel Puliatti.*

This change is an example of the way many of Wright's female clients were able to get him to alter some of the features of his original house plans to suit their needs, though often quite reluctantly, as was the case with both the Walker and Barnsdall Houses. (As I documented in a 2014 article in *Western Art and Architecture Magazine*, Wright worked with several independent and strong-willed female clients during his career who usually got him to accept their preferences.) Wright ended up accommodating Elizabeth's request by raising the height of ceiling on the north side so the overhanging eaves would not cut off the view.

The ceiling in most of the living room is seven feet, ten inches tall, with wooden panels between open beaming. Wright was only five feet, seven inches tall, and most of his ceiling heights were somewhat lower than the average heights in other houses at that time. At the north end, the ceiling is two feet higher, with a plain glass clerestory running east to west around the edge of this raised section. A fireplace faced with concrete blocks is set into the east wall, and there are built-in bookshelves lining the northeast corner of the room. There is also a low built-in seat that runs along the wall between the fireplace and the northeast corner. Most of these features are shown in the scenes set inside the Pearce House in *Permanent Midnight*.

At the west end of this open multiuse space is a wood-sided service core that rises from floor to ceiling, with cabinets set into it and built-in shelves lining the north side. The kitchen, or "workspace" as Wright's plans labeled it, is quite small. Wright's Usonian kitchens were usually small, which is a clear indication that he did not feel these spaces were as important as other common rooms. Here Wright used mahogany overlay cabinets and countertops. To the left of the service core is a long gallery that runs almost the length of the south side of the house. The outer wall is made of floor-to-ceiling windows, creating a pleasing indoor-outdoor effect and bathing the interior with natural light. The gallery, a feature found in most of Wright's Usonian homes, connects the two bedrooms: a small bedroom in the middle of the house and master bedroom suite at the far west end.

The supervising architect for the Pearce House was Aaron Green, one of Wright's most trusted associates from his Taliesin Studio. Green reoriented Wright's original placement of the house to avoid the steepest part of its hillside lot and allow for more space for the workshop and studio wing off the east end. Wilbur and Elizabeth Pearce occupied the home until their deaths, and their son Llewellyn moved in in 1985. Then their grandson Konrad Pearce gained title to the property in 2002. Soon afterward he began making plans to restore his grandparents' elegant house to its original condition.

The gallery inside the Pearce House. *Photo by Joel Puliatti.*

As of this writing, Konrad's work has been delayed by the pandemic and financial constraints. He plans to begin with electrical, plumbing and roof repairs and then move on to restoring the living areas soon after.

Permanent Midnight (1998)

This intense film is a case study in how too much money and easy access to drugs can ruin your life. It has been described by viewers as a tragedy, a comedy, disturbing or sad. At various points in the story, it is each of those things. It was a total bomb at the box office. But it did get some praise from critics for Ben Stiller's performance as the real-life drug addict Jerry Stahl. His starring role in *Permanent Midnight* was far removed from the comical doofuses he had recently played, in a cameo in *Happy Gilmore* and in the films *The Cable Guy* and *There's Something About Mary*. The Wilbur Pearce House features prominently throughout the film as the residence of Stahl's wife, Sandra, and later his home as well.

The movie was based on the autobiography of the same name by highly successful Los Angeles TV writer Jerry Stahl, who worked on such popular shows as *Thirtysomething*, *Twin Peaks* and *ALF*. In the opening line, Ben Stiller's voiceover on a black screen tells us, "Smack is like the leisure suit of the '90s." In one of the first scenes, he tells a woman he meets during his rehab phase (played by Maria Bello) that he took drugs because, "In Hollywood—you gotta look your best!" As the story unfolds, we slowly learn how much Jerry has lost due to his drug addiction.

About seven minutes into the movie, Jerry is introduced to Sandra by his "drug buddy" Nicky, played by Owen Wilson. Sandra, played by Elizabeth Hurley, is a British citizen who works for the producer of a popular TV comedy called *Mr. Chompers*, an adult-sized sarcastic alien puppet. She lives in the Pearce House and Jerry and Nicky meet her there at night. They sit and talk in the living room, with the magnificent view of the lights of greater LA visible outside the wall of windows along the south side. According to Konrad Pearce, while the exterior of the house was used for all of the outdoor scenes, a set had to be created for the interior scenes. He told me this was because the interior was not in good condition at the time *Permanent Midnight* was being filmed, due to damage from a long-term tenant and years of deferred maintenance. So, the production company re-created the original appearance of the interior using Wright's plans and old photos. At the end of this scene,

Ben Stiller having a meltdown in *Permanent Midnight.*

Jerry agrees to marry Sandra to help her get a green card, and she promises to get him an interview with her producer to write for *Mr. Chompers.*

The next day, Jerry gets hired to rewrite a poorly written script for the *Mr. Chompers* show. That episode is a hit with viewers, and Jerry and Sandra are shown a few scenes later watching it in bed in the master bedroom of her house after they were married. He gets out of bed to go to the bathroom to secretly take Percodan pills. When he comes out, she asks him to move in with her, but he puts her off, revealing that she is falling for Jerry while he remains aloof, being more interested in getting high than in a serious relationship.

Twenty-five minutes into the film, Jerry returns to Sandra's house after attending his mother's funeral back east and asks if he can move in with her. The next morning, after she leaves for work at seven o'clock, he gets up two hours later and goes to the bathroom to shoot up, causing him to arrive late at his new job in a disheveled state and obviously high. All his coworkers are embarrassed by his behavior, including Sandra, but they don't say anything about it.

Jerry's total meltdown occurs in the next scene at the Pearce House during a party Sandra throws to celebrate Jerry's getting a big book deal from an agent she had introduced him to. Sandra catches Jerry in her bathroom shooting up, and in her anger over his not going to rehab like he promised, she tells him her boss is firing him from his show. When he asks why, she says, "Because he can't work with you anymore! You're always late to work and coming in stoned!" Jerry ignores her displeasure and joins the party. But a few minutes later, we see him go back to the bathroom to shoot up again. This time he starts hallucinating, thinking he sees *Mr. Chompers* trying to force his way into the bathroom while Jerry tries to keep him out. He begins to shout at the giant puppet, who shouts back at him that he's "a lousy writer" because he cares more about feeding his drug addiction than writing. After a tug-of-war between them at the bathroom door, Jerry finally breaks free, stumbles into the living room and then turns around and vomits in the toilet with the door still open, shocking his guests. While this scene might seem comical to some viewers, it's clearly not funny to Jerry or Sandra.

In the next scene, he confesses to Kitty, "It was getting to the point where I had to shoot six bags just to turn on the typewriter." In the next flashback, we see him at home with Sandra, sneaking out of the living room and going down the gallery to find the drugs he's hidden in the master bedroom. When he can't find them, Sandra walks in and tells him, "I threw them away." He begs her to let him get high "one last time." She says she'll give him back his drugs and help him get an interview for a job on another TV show if he starts attending a rehab program "in the morning." He promises, and she is relieved, telling him, "I really *do* love you."

Jerry manages to get the new TV writing job, even though he's clearly stoned again at the interview. He does go to register at an outpatient rehab

Ben Stiller and Elizabeth Hurley in the gallery of the Pearce House in *Permanent Midnight*. This was a set on a sound stage.

center, but in the parking lot he meets a drug dealer, who becomes his supplier for even stronger doses of heroin. He lies about this to Sandra and manages to hide his continuing addiction from her and the fact that he gets fired from his new job after a few weeks. One day after spending the afternoon with his new drug buddy, he comes home and finds Sandra working at her typewriter on a new script. She stops to tell him she's pregnant, and instead of being happy to hear this news, he says nothing and walks back to their bedroom to shoot up. When she walks in and catches him with a needle in his arm, she explodes and drags him down the hallway, shouting, "I don't ever want to see you again!" before shoving him out the front door.

Most of the last half hour of *Permanent Midnight* depicts Jerry's rapidly deteriorating life after he loses Sandra, including his estrangement from his newborn daughter after Sandra agrees to let him see her occasionally. The exterior of the Pearce House is shown one final time, when Jerry visits Sandra to say he's sorry for how he treated her. But the story does not end there, with Jerry trying to start a new chapter in his life.

This film received a score of 59 percent on Rotten Tomatoes. Reactions by movie critics were mixed, with some praising Stiller's performance. Michael O' Sullivan of *The Washington Post* felt that "as Stahl, Stiller turns in what could easily be the finest performance of a career that, up to now, was devoted to playing an interesting but lightweight assortment of dweebs—this arresting performance—is a breakthrough for the talented actor." Roger Ebert gave this film three stars, saying, "The movie gets credit for not making the high life seem colorful or funny. It is not. It is boring, because when the drugs are there, they simply clear the pain and allow the mind to focus on getting more drugs." Anyone who has watched a family member or a friend descend into drug addiction can attest to the truth of that observation.

Film Facts

Director: David Veloz
Studio: Artisan Entertainment
Release Date: September 12, 1998
Stars: Ben Stiller, Elizabeth Hurley, Maria Bello, Owen Wilson, Janeane Garofalo, Cheryl Ladd
Running Time: 88 minutes
Budget: unknown
Box Office Gross: $1,171,999 (Canada and United States)

4

CANNIBAL WOMEN CHASE BILL MAHER AROUND A MILLIONAIRE COMMUNIST'S HOUSE

THE BARNSDALL (HOLLYHOCK) HOUSE, 4808 HOLLYWOOD BOULEVARD, LOS ANGELES

To say Aline Barnsdall was an unusual woman would be an understatement. She was an oil heiress who inherited enough income from her father's oil wells to indulge her passion for the theater and hire America's leading architect to design a complex of buildings that included a residence for her and her daughter, a state-of-the art theater and apartments for actors. She planned to eventually include commercial shops, artists' studios and a movie theater. She was also a devout supporter of the Communist Revolution in Russia and was a close friend of the famed American anarchist and socialist Emma Goldman. She chose never to marry but gave birth to her daughter Betty by a live-in lover and raised the child by herself. Her residence, now known as the Hollyhock House, was used as a setting for the 1989 film *Cannibal Women in the Avocado Jungle of Death*. Today, this residence is open to the public as a city landmark called The Hollyhock House, nicknamed after Aline Barnsdall's favorite flower, which inspired the use of hollyhock-shaped finials along the exterior.

The Hollywood Hills were still mostly open grassland when Aline Barnsdall bought a thirty-six-acre tract called Olive Hill in 1919 on a hilltop above Hollywood Boulevard just west of Vermont Avenue. The village of Hollywood had been incorporated into the city of Los Angeles in 1910. The first motion picture to be filmed there, *In Old California*, directed by D.W. Griffith while working for Biograph Company, had begun production that year. The Hollywood Hills remained largely undeveloped until the first residential tract was laid out in 1918.

Aline Barnsdall with her daughter Betty, 1922. *Courtesy of Bison Archives.*

Barnsdall first approached Frank Lloyd Wright in 1915 in Chicago, where she was living then and was a patron of an avant-garde theater company. She asked Wright to design a state-of-the art theater for this company, which staged controversial plays. Aline soon changed her mind and asked Wright to design a performing arts complex for her in Los Angeles, where she had moved in 1916. She chose Wright because of his reputation as a progressive architect and his well-known love for the arts, including theater and motion pictures. Los Angeles was a boom town in the 1910s, drawing new residents from all over the country. Between 1910 and 1920, the population of Los Angeles grew from 300,000 to nearly 600,000, and the city was attracting educated professionals and artists. This included Wright himself and his son Lloyd, who opened his own successful architecture practice there in 1915, while the elder Wright moved his office to Los Angeles in 1923. The two would collaborate on several residential commissions around Southern California during those years, including the home that the elder Wright designed for Aline Barnsdall. After living in Los Angeles for two years, Wright sarcastically stated, "Tip the world over on its side, and everything loose will end up in Los Angeles." Yet his dedication to completing the seven commissions he designed in the LA area (including a group of shops in Beverly Hills) belies that sentiment.

At the time Wright first met Barnsdall, he had already begun incorporating elements of Pre-Columbian Indigenous architecture into some of his designs, especially those from Mayan temples in the jungles of Central America. Wright had been intrigued with Mayan and Aztec architecture since his mid-twenties, when he had seen ersatz examples of such buildings at the World's Columbian Exposition in Chicago in 1893. He used some of these motifs in his design for a warehouse for the A.D. German Company in Richland Center, Wisconsin, in 1915. The upper portion of the walls on this warehouse clearly display geometric decorations that were inspired by temples in Chichén Itzá on the Yucatán Peninsula in Mexico. That same year, Wright drew the plans for the Imperial Hotel in Tokyo, which also had Mayan motifs around the main entrance.

Wright completed his first set of drawings for Aline Barnsdall's house in 1917 with three possible styles: Prairie, Neo-Gothic or Pre-Columbian. Barnsdall chose the last style. But the journey from these drawings to the actual construction of the buildings on Olive Hill would be a long and difficult one, filled with construction difficulties, communication problems and design changes that would test both the working relationship and friendship between Wright and his mercurial client. The top of Olive Hill was a difficult site for building such a grandiose complex. Although it had unimpeded views of downtown Los Angeles, the San Gabriel Mountains to the north and the Pacific Ocean to the west, it was quite isolated from the commercial center of Los Angeles and the rest of Hollywood. It was also windswept and dusty. This made it difficult to transport building materials and work crews to the site, contributing to construction delays. But there were also traumas in Wright's personal life during the time he worked with Barnsdall.

The period between 1915, when Wright met Barnsdall, and 1924, when she finally gave up on her dream of completing her grand project, was an especially difficult phase in Wright's personal and professional life. In 1914, he had lost both his lover and his Wisconsin home and studio, Taliesin East, to a fire and horrific multiple murder. His lover, Mamah Cheney, her two children and four house guests were butchered by a deranged servant who had set the house on fire while Wright was giving a lecture in Milwaukee. In 1915, Wright began a romance with a divorcée named Miriam while he was still legally married to his first wife. He would eventually marry Miriam, but their on-again, off-again relationship led to angry letters from Miriam to Wright being published in several major newspapers. Six months after they married in 1923, Miriam left Wright for good. During those same years, Wright was also working on several commissions while staying in Japan, including the Imperial Hotel and a girls' school. The public scrutiny Wright endured from his scandals, and the time he was away in Japan, distracted him from his work. On top of all this, some critics were stating publicly that he was out of touch with the new minimalist styles coming out of Europe and that his work was hopelessly romantic and outdated. While such criticism seems ludicrous in hindsight, these comments took a real toll on Wright's

The concrete finials at Hollyhock House. *Photo by Joel Puliatti.*

career, as evidenced by the fact that Barnsdall was his only American client from 1918 to 1921.

Construction on Barnsdall's complex began in 1919, with her residence being completed first. She had Wright place her house at the top of Olive Hill, with its spectacular views of the LA Basin. Wright had to redraw his plans, since he had assumed that the live theater would be in this spot, which was one of several design changes required by Barnsdall that would cause strains in their relationship and lead to budget issues between them. During the time Wright was in Japan, he had his son Lloyd act as the supervising architect at the site. The house was constructed of hollow clay tiles covered by stucco over a wood balloon frame. The ornamental hollyhock finials along the upper walls were made of cast concrete. The use of hollow clay tiles for load-bearing walls was an experimental technique at the time. Wright did not employ his new textile block method until four years later, when he built the Millard House in Pasadena.

The Hollyhock House is a two-story, six-thousand-square-foot T-shaped residence with seven bedrooms, seven bathrooms, a large living room, a formal dining room, a kitchen, a music room, a library, a conservatory and an enclosed sunporch. Wright placed the living room on the western side, behind the entrance loggia at a right angle to the music room and library. The other major rooms are arranged around a central open "garden court." There is another walled patio off the south end of the house, with a small reflecting pool in front of the west entrance and a children's reflecting pool with terraced seating around the edges at the eastern end. These features are prominent settings for scenes in *Cannibal Women in the Avocado Jungle of Death.* Wright also designed a nearby pergola and a row of kennels running off the northeast corner of the house, both of which survive intact.

The living room is dominated by a massive concrete chimney that rises up through the ceiling, which is two feet higher at the corners of the chimney to emphasize its visual impact. A large skylight above the fireplace has a decorative pattern of geometric wood framing. The over mantel is embellished with an intricate design of interlocking circles and triangles reminiscent of paintings by Vassily Kandinsky. Wright placed a small concrete pool in the floor in front of the fireplace to reflect the flames when the fireplace was used at night. Another advanced feature of the Barnsdall House was the use of rhythmic patterns in the leaded casements on the bay windows and in the hallways. Along the wide square bay in the nursery room, the wood-framed leaded windows have zigzag and chevron patterns that are several years ahead of their time in anticipating the Art Deco style, which first appeared in Europe in the mid-1920s. Wright's innovative use of such geometric patterns can also be seen on the concrete finials with stylized hollyhock motifs that give a distinctly Art Deco–like appearance to the outer walls all around the house.

One of the most aesthetically pleasing elements of Hollyhock House is Wright's use of rich oakwood paneling along the walls of the living room, dining room and the hallways, which gives these rooms a warm, pleasing ambience. The framing of the floor-to-ceiling windows and doors along the loggia facing the courtyard are also made of the same wood. There is a distinct Arts-and-Crafts quality to this use of undisguised natural materials, and Wright was one of the first American architects to incorporate such design features into his residential work.

In 1920, Barnsdall asked Wright to design two guesthouses for her on Olive Hill, which were called Residence A and Residence B. Residence B was demolished in 1948, but Residence A still stands, one of the few examples of Wright's Prairie style on the West Coast. Wright never completed plans for the theater building Barnsdall wanted. Despite this, she asked him to design a schoolhouse for her daughter and other children in 1923, down the hill from Hollyhock House. Construction on the school was never completed because City of Los Angeles inspectors cited it for alleged code violations. Its foundation was later used by the Austrian architect Rudolph Schindler to build an open-air play space. After construction on the school was halted, Barnsdall fired Wright from the project, and he threatened to sue her for his unpaid bills. These issues were eventually settled out of court, and Wright and Barnsdall finally reconciled and resumed their friendship. Aline died in 1946 while she was living in Residence B.

In 1924, Barnsdall offered to give Hollyhock House, the two guesthouses and eleven acres on Olive Hill to the City of Los Angeles. The city finally accepted her offer in 1927 after she hired Schindler to complete the upstairs rooms of her residence. Over the next sixty-seven years, the property was used as the headquarters of the California Art Club, a USO facility, a social club called the Olive Hill Foundation and an art gallery. Then the house sat empty for many years. The 1994 Northridge Earthquake did extensive damage to all the buildings on Olive Hill. FEMA initiated a restoration project, with added funding from the City of Los Angeles and the state. Hollyhock House was open to the public from 2005 until 2010 and then closed again for further repairs due to water damage from the leaky flat roof Wright designed, a common problem with all his flat-roofed houses. In 2015, Hollyhock House was reopened for tours.

The living room of Hollyhock House. *Photo by Joel Puliatti.*

Hollyhock House was designated a Los Angeles Historic Monument by the city in 1963. In 1971, the Barnsdall Complex was added to the National Register of Historic Places. In 2007, it was declared a National Historic Landmark. And in July 2019, Hollyhock House, along with seven other Wright-designed buildings, was added to the UNESCO World Heritage List as part of a special category called "The 20th-Century Architecture of Frank Lloyd Wright." It is the only California site to be so honored. Jeffrey Herr, the former curator of Hollyhock House, summed up its importance by writing, "Its use of indoor/outdoor spaces marks it as a prototype of the modern ranch house."

Cannibal Women in the Avocado Jungle of Death (1989)

This parody of Indiana Jones–type adventure films has become a true cult classic. At the time of its release, many viewers condemned it as sexually exploitive or a badly written story with absurd characters and dialogue. But in recent years, it has garnered a more appreciative audience who recognize its deliberate over-the-top humor and preposterous scenarios as a send-up of famous "adventure" films that have portrayed similar narratives in jungle settings. It is also a partial exception to the criteria used for including films in this book. It is a feature film that was released by a major studio but did not have a theatrical release the year it was made, going straight to home video. However, it *has* been screened in multiple theaters and viewed by live audiences since then. Some critics claim the movie was a spoof of Joseph Conrad's 1899 novella *Heart of Darkness*, but the similarities are superficial.

The story revolves around a plan by the U.S. military, which decides to send an expedition to protect America's dwindling supply of avocados by traveling to the "Avocado Jungle." This is a mysterious tropical zone ludicrously located in the Central Valley of California, which ranges from "Bakersfield to the Mexican border," according to U.S. intelligence. To lead this expedition, the government chooses a prominent feminist professor from "Spritzer College" named Margo, played by Shannon Tweed. Margo asks one of her adoring students, Bunny, to join her to give her experience in doing "fieldwork," even though Bunny is portrayed as a well-meaning bimbo. This expedition will have to locate the fearsome "Piranha Women," who think men are only good as a source of food and like to eat them with guacamole dip made from their ample supply of the fruit in their jungle kingdom. The military wants Margo to convince these cannibal women to relocate to condos on a reservation in Malibu so the government can access their avocados and overcome an "avocado gap" with the Soviet Union. From there, the plot becomes even sillier.

Margo realizes they will need an experienced guide on this expedition to navigate the challenging terrain and ward off any dangers that might lurk in the avocado jungle. So, she stops at an inn before heading for the jungle and ends up considering several weird applicants. She finally hires Jim, an unabashed chauvinist she had a one-night stand with (played by Bill Maher four years before he hosted his first TV show, *Politically Incorrect*). During the drive to the avocado jungle, Margo describes her brief affair with Jim to Bunny, and when Bunny seems surprised that her mentor would be attracted to such a man, Margo replies, "Modern feminists don't eat men—at least not since the '60s."

After the group has trekked deep into the jungle, they meet a tribe of subservient men who gather around campfires at night chanting the names of famous "sensitive men" like Alan Alda, Walter Mondale and Mark Harmon. When Margo praises this tribe, Jim accuses her of wanting to "dominate men" and tries to get the tribe to do masculine things like drinking beer and belching loudly. Later, when Margo's group finally encounters a hunting party of Piranha Women after a long canoe trip along an Amazon-like river, Margo shows them her NOW membership card to placate them and asks to be taken to their leader. In the next scene, about fifty-four minutes into the film, we see the west façade of Hollyhock House as the cannibal women lead Margo's group toward the building while she says, "This must be the secret temple of the Piranha Women." When they get closer, Margo comments, "Their architecture is surprisingly advanced." But Jim looks askance, then jokes, "Really? It looks like a big Lego to me." Most of the remaining thirty-five minutes of the film take place in and around Hollyhock House.

Margo's group is led into the central courtyard, where she speculates, "This must be the altar space where they eat guys!" Jim then looks over at the small reflecting pool in the center of the courtyard with its reddish water and piranhas swimming in it. He assumes this must be where the cannibal women throw the bodies of the men they eat to have their bones picked clean. Then the leader of the Piranha Women appears atop the parapet above the courtyard with some of her bodyguards. Margo recognizes her as a former feminist professor named Dr. Kurtz, played by Adrienne Barbeau.

Opposite, top: South façade of Hollyhock House, as seen in *Cannibal Women in the Avocado Jungle of Death*, headquarters of the Cannibal Women.

Opposite, middle: Bill Maher outside Hollyhock House after being captured by the Cannibal Women.

Opposite, bottom: Bill Maher and Shannon Tweed (*on the left*) looking at the piranha pool outside Hollyhock House.

Above: Adrienne Barbeau, leader of the Cannibal Women, standing between the hollyhock finials.

Margo is surprised that Dr. Kurtz has joined these cannibal women, telling her, "Eating prisoners is a serious breach of ethics!" Dr. Kurtz replies, "The future of feminism lies in this temple," adding, "This is a war between men and women!" She tells Margo that there is no avocado shortage, and the U.S. military just wants her tribe to relocate to Malibu condos to convert them into "beach bunnies." She asks Margo to take her rightful place among feminists and join the Piranha Women. When she refuses, Dr. Kurtz orders her warriors to seize Margo and her companions and take them inside Hollyhock House, where they will all spend the next twenty-four hours awaiting their fate.

During the courtyard scene, close-up shots of the hollyhock finials behind Dr Kurtz are shown several times as she looks down on her captives, which could be seen as a not-so-subtle Freudian metaphor for a row of phallic symbols, now dominated by strong women. The next several scenes are set mostly in various bedrooms and smaller sitting rooms inside Hollyhock House, where Margo and Bunny deal with attempts to convince them to join the Piranha Women and Jim tries to avoid being marinated before being eaten by them.

Cannibal Women in the Avocado Jungle of Death received a 50 percent rating from viewers on Rotten Tomatoes. Critics' reactions were mixed, with those written years after its release being more positive than negative. The reviewer for *The Digital Fix*, Anthony Nield, wrote in 2012, "*Cannibal Women* is a pretty smart film, with Lawton's screenplay among its major qualities." The review in *TV Guide* concluded, "This film is not nearly as bad as it might have been, thanks largely to the leads. Moreover, *Cannibal Women* does manage to be on target with its humor from time to time." Julian White, in a review for the British magazine *Starburst*, called the film "a light-hearted romp," and added, "True, the constant ribbing at feminists seems very dated, but it's never mean-spirited, and anyway the girls give as good as they get."

Film Facts

Director: J.F. Lawton
Studio: Guacamole Films for Paramount Home Video
Release Date: March 15, 1989
Stars: Bill Maher, Shannon Tweed, Adrienne Barbeau
Running Time: 90 minutes
Budget: not recorded
Box Office Gross: unknown

5

FROM *WESTWORLD* TO *DEEP SPACE NINE*

THE MILLARD HOUSE (LA MINIATURA), 645 PROSPECT CRESCENT, PASADENA

The first residence Wright designed using his textile block method was the Alice Millard House in Pasadena, designed in 1923 and completed in 1925. This was also the first example of Wright's use of his Mayan temple style for houses. The solid massing of the house, its setback lines, geometric patterns along the walls and the blending of the building into its almost jungle-like setting combine to create the effect of a well-preserved Mayan temple when viewed from the curb. The Millard House is set well back from the street down a tree-shaded path, and the feeling this romantic composition creates is simply magical. Two popular TV series included episodes that used the Millard House as a setting: *Westworld* and *Star Trek: Deep Space Nine.*

Alice and her husband, George, met Wright when he still lived in Illinois and hired him to design a wood-frame Prairie style house for them in Highland Park in 1906. Alice imported and sold antique furnishings and rare books. After her husband died, Alice decided to relocate to Southern California, where she hired Wright to design an all-concrete house that he nicknamed La Miniatura, Spanish for "The Miniature." Although the Millard House may not seem to be small to most people at two thousand square feet, it was not one of Wright's larger Southern California residences. Wright's use of the secluded, lushly landscaped lot at the end of a cul-de-sac, where he set the house well back from the street on the cusp of a small ravine, was simply masterful. Standing outside the house and taking in the semitropical setting, one can completely forget that they are in the middle of a modern American city of nearly 140,000 people.

Concrete was a material Wright had begun experimenting with in the early 1900s, first using it on the Unity Temple in Oak Park, Illinois, in 1904. After he moved to Los Angeles in 1923, he developed his textile block adaptation of concrete construction, being the first architect to use this method on a large scale for residences. All four of the textile block houses that Wright designed in greater Los Angeles still stand, although there were construction and maintenance problems with this system in each of these homes, including roof leakage and flooding in the basement. In the case of the Millard House, Wright was criticized and even ridiculed by local critics and rival architects for these problems. In 2005, a *New York Times* article describing the Millard House mused, "What kind of rich person, many wondered, would want to live in such a house?" since concrete was a material many considered appropriate only for bridges and large commercial buildings in the early twentieth century. However, Wright was quite proud of his work, saying after it was completed, "I would rather have built that little house than St. Peter's in Rome." He added that his design for the Millard House "belonged to the ground on which it stood." Anyone visiting this house today would surely agree.

The entrance to the Millard House is on the side of the home, facing north. The double front doors have redwood-framed glass panels. Upon entering the house, visitors emerge from the low ceiling of the entryway into an impressive two-story living room, a classic example of Wright's "compression and release design" technique. This spacious room has a fifteen-foot-high ceiling lined with redwood beams and paneling. Along the west wall of this room, Wright placed a row of wood-framed, glass-paneled doors that open onto a concrete balcony overlooking the secluded garden behind the home. This garden is heavily wooded along its sides, and there is a romantic-looking man-made pond in the middle. The walls of the living room are made out of concrete blocks, which are set into plain square panels along the south wall. Above the doors Wright placed clear glass transoms, and above these are four rows of concrete panels with cutout geometric designs in a cross pattern. Set into the eastern wall of the living room is a walk-in fireplace with concrete block facing. This wall is topped by a balcony that runs along an opening to the second story, providing an impressive view of the magnificent living room below.

Many visitors to the Millard House assume that the cross motifs incised or pierced into the textile blocks along the walls are Wright's version of the traditional Christian cross. Actually, Wright adapted this particular design from Navajo rug patterns. In fact, his use of such motifs was inspired by the

The living room of the Millard House. *Photo by Joel Puliatti.*

Redwood front door at the Millard House, with Wright's cross motif pattern. *Photo by Joel Puliatti.*

The Millard House, with the guesthouse and lagoon. *Photo by Joel Puliatti.*

various Indigenous Native American cultures in North and Central America, which he admired and used as inspiration for many of his residential design features from the 1910s on.

There is a spacious, well-lit bedroom on the east end of the entry level with a twelve-foot-high ceiling and tall, narrow windows on the eastern wall that catch the morning light. All the floors in the main house, as well as the guesthouse/studio in the backyard, are made of concrete slabs in a four-foot-square pattern, the same pattern Wright would use on his mid-century Usonian houses throughout the United States. Between this bedroom and the living room is a set of stairs that leads down to the formal dining room on the bottom level. The walls of the dining room are made of plain concrete, and there's a small fireplace on the east wall. On the west wall, Wright placed French doors leading to a concrete patio, which adjoins the garden. Behind the dining room is the kitchen, with an adjoining pantry in the southeast corner and a maid's room on the northeast corner.

On the third level of the Millard House, Wright placed the master bedroom suite. This bedroom has a peaceful, pleasing ambience, with its floor-to-ceiling wood-latticed windows overlooking the wooded front yard and a fourteen-foot ceiling. Here, the large windows that open outward, sylvan views and ample natural light create the indoor-outdoor effect that Wright was so famous for. The master bath has Delft tiles along the walls and an eighteenth-century Italian carved wood door, which are some of the antique features that Millard asked Wright to incorporate into his design. The fourth level of the house has a wide concrete deck with a low wall along its perimeter and a sleeping loft along the east side. The deck provides marvelous views of the entire property.

A concrete footpath runs along the northern edge of the garden and connects the main house to a two-story guesthouse and studio. This was included in Wright's original plans, but the actual design and construction of this building was carried out by his son Lloyd Wright, in 1926. He included his father's design motifs from the main house: textile block construction and the same geometric patterns pierced or incised into the walls around the front entrance, which faces the garden, with tall, glass-paned doors that open outward. The main room is a spacious living room/library on the entry level, with fifteen-foot-high two-story ceilings and an adjoining dining room and pantry. Off the east end is a cozy sitting room with a fireplace faced in concrete blocks. On the upper level are a bedroom and full bath. There is another entrance to the studio on this level, up a set of outside stairs. This door opens onto an interior balcony that overlooks the living room. In 2001,

Frank Lloyd Wright's grandson Eric Wright supervised a through restoration of both the main house and the guesthouse.

The original budget Wright gave Alice Millard for the construction of La Miniatura was $10,000. But like most of his other residential commissions, the final cost was much more: in this case, $17,000. Wright used local sand from the building site for the concrete blocks, as he did with his other textile block houses. He believed this would ensure the color and texture of the blocks would blend in with the natural setting of each house. Yet in practice, this system created several problems. The color and texture of the finished concrete blocks did not always match that of the sand at the site. Also, the impurities of the local sand led to deterioration of the concrete blocks over time, as well as greater damage from water leakage. Thus, the same solutions that owners of Wright's houses have adopted for such problems were applied by the owners of the Millard House over the years: regular, diligent maintenance and replacement of failing materials as needed, just as is required for most older homes.

The entire Millard property, including the main house and the guesthouse, was placed on the National Register of Historic Places in December 1976. The Millard House sold in 2008 for $7 million and again in 2009 for $5 million. The property was last listed for sale in 2013 for $4.5 million and was finally sold to a private buyer for an undisclosed price in May 2015.

Westworld (2018 and 2022)

Westworld was an innovative and popular TV series on HBO that ran for four seasons between 2016 and 2022. Two episodes each from season two (2018) and season three (2020) had scenes that were filmed at the Millard House. It was used as the residence of one of the main characters, Arnold Weber. This series was based on the 1973 dystopian/science fiction/fantasy film *Westworld*, which was written and directed by Michael Crichton, and depicts a high-tech theme park where robots are created to look like various Wild West characters and act as hosts for visitors. These robots begin behaving erratically and eventually go completely out of control.

In the HBO TV series, the Millard House first appears in episode 2, titled "Reunion," in the second season. As this episode begins, two of the pivotal characters are talking in the living room of a modern house at night. They are Dolores Abernathy, played by Evan Rachel Wood, and Bernard Lowe, played by Jeffrey Wright. Dolores is a host dressed like a farmer's daughter. Like all the hosts from Westworld, she has become sentient and is starting to remember events from her time working in the theme park. As she talks to Bernard, the head of programming for Westworld, he tries to help her by explaining she is not in the theme park anymore or having a dream but is now in "our world"—in other words, the real world. As she listens, she looks out over the night skyline of an undisclosed city. The voice of Dr. Robert Ford, played by Anthony Hopkins, can be heard in the background, asking if Dolores is "ready yet." Dr. Ford is the scientist who altered the settings of some hosts to make then sentient. Bernard tells him she's not ready yet to fully function in the real world. Then Dolores comments, "Have you ever seen anything so full of splendor?" as she gazes at the lights of the city. Bernard is touched by her childlike sense of wonder and tells her most people in the real world simply stop noticing such sights.

About three minutes into the episode, Bernard takes Dolores outside and walks her over to the site of a new house that is being built for Bernard and his family. This is likely a set that re-creates part of the exterior of the Millard House, with unfinished rooms beyond the entrance. The site is at the edge of the downtown area, and the lights of the skyscrapers in the distance are probably a CGI creation. Dolores and Bernard walk through the open façade of the house and past piles of construction materials, including textile blocks lining the unfinished walls and stacked along the floors,

Evan Rachel Wood and Jeffrey Wright outside his future home. The structure was likely a set, and the skyline was created with CGI.

Above: The Charles Ennis House in the Hollywood Hills, used as a location for over a dozen feature films. *Photo by Joel Puliatti.*

Left: Poster from the 1959 film *House on Haunted Hill*, showing Vincent Price and his "haunted house" above, which vaguely resembles the Ennis House, where this movie was filmed.

Top: The Della Walker House. This was one of Wright's Usonian-style houses adapted to a beach setting. It was a location for the 1959 movie *A Summer Place*. *Photo by Joel Puliatti.*

Bottom: Richard Egan, Troy Donahue and Sandra Dee outside the Walker House during the filming of *A Summer Place*.

Top: Scene from *A Summer Place* showing Dorothy McGuire walking down a "staircase" inside the Walker House. This was a set created to give the house a lower story.

Bottom: The actual interior of the Walker House, which is a single-story cottage. *Photo by Joel Puliatti*.

Scene from the 1989 movie *Black Rain*, showing the north façade of the Ennis House on a rainy night, with a distinctly bluish hue. Director Ridley Scott's creative use of lighting elicits an ominous feeling as Michael Douglas's character is about to enter the home of a Japanese yakuza boss.

Tomisaburô Wakayama in *Black Rain* in the living room of the Ennis House as he explains the meaning of the phrase black rain. Ridley Scott's use of an eerie orange glow accentuates the yakuza boss's passion.

Scene from the 1982 movie *Blade Runner* with Harrison Ford at his apartment inside the Ennis House. This was a set on a sound stage used to control lighting conditions during filming.

The Aline Barnsdall House, known as Hollyhock House. This was a location for the 1989 film *Cannibal Women in the Avocado Jungle of Death*. When Bill Maher's character first sees the house he says, "It looks like a giant Lego to me." *Photo by Joel Puliatti.*

Scene from *Cannibal Women* in the courtyard of Hollyhock House, with Shannon Tweed looking up at Adrienne Barbeau, leader of the cannibal women tribe, standing between the hollyhock finials.

Scene from *Cannibal Women* with Bill Maher and Shannon Tweed in the courtyard of Hollyhock House as he discovers the bloody pool where the tribe members throw the bones of the men they have captured after they eat them.

Scene from the 1998 movie *Permanent Midnight*, with Ben Stiller and Owen Wilson in the living room of the Wilbur Pearce House. This was a set built to avoid possible damage to the real house and control lighting conditions.

The actual living room of the Pearce House, looking north toward the San Gabriel Mountains. *Photo by Joel Puliatti.*

Top: Scene from the 1991 movie *The Rocketeer* with Jennifer Connelly trying to escape from Timothy Dalton's house where she was held after being kidnaped. This was likely a set that re-created a bedroom wing of the Ennis House.

Bottom: Scene from the 1998 movie *Rush Hour*, with Jackie Chan in the living room of the John Snowden house talking to the niece of his good friend at their home in "Hong Kong."

Opposite, top: Scene from the 1997 film *Gattaca* with Ethan Hawke walking along the upper corridor of the main hallway of the Marin County Civic Center Administration Building.

Opposite, bottom: The upper corridor of the Main County Civic Center Administration Building, the only government facility designed by Wright that was ever built. *Photo by Joel Puliatti.*

The rooftops of the Marin County Civic Center Administration Building. The blue color was chosen to replace Wright's original choice of gold because gold paint would tarnish quickly. *Photo by Joel Puliatti.*

Scene from *Gattaca* with Ethan Hawke working as a janitor while longing to go into outer space while he watches a rocket launch from a nearby spaceport.

Scene from the 1975 movie *The Day of the Locust*, with Richard Dysart and William Atherton standing on the deck of the Ennis House with a view overlooking downtown Los Angeles.

Scene from *The Day of the Locust* with William Atherton standing in front of the large leaded window in the living room of the Ennis House, realizing that he sold out his integrity to keep his job at a movie studio.

Opposite, top: The John Storer House living room, one of Wright's four textile block houses in the LA area. This house was painstakingly restored by noted Hollywood producer Joel Silver. *Photo by Joel Puliatti.*

Opposite, bottom: The Arch Oboler Compound, Malibu, view of gatehouse and main residence. This complex burned down in the 2018 Woolsey Fire, leaving only the foundations of each building. *Photo by Joel Puliatti.*

Right: Poster from the 1951 movie *Bwana Devil*, the first feature-length color 3-D film, which was produced by Arch Oboler while he lived at his Malibu compound.

Below: Eleanor's Retreat at the Oboler Compound, built for Arch Oboler's wife. This was the main location for the 1951 dystopian movie *Five*, written, produced and directed by Oboler. *Photo by Joel Puliatti.*

Top: Scene from Alfred Hitchcock's 1959 thriller *North by Northwest*, with Cary Grant walking toward the home of the arch villain Phillip Vandamm. The story behind its creation surprises many viewers.

Bottom: Scene from the 1971 dystopian movie *THX 1138*, George Lucas's first feature film. This is a combination of the main hallway of the Marin County Civic Center's Administration Building on the right, and CGI images on the left.

Opposite, top: The living room of the guesthouse at La Miniatura, the Millard House in Pasadena, which is the home of Jeffrey Wright's character in the TV series *Westworld*. *Photo by Joel Puliatti.*

Opposite, bottom: Jeffrey Wright walking past the lagoon in front of the guesthouse at La Miniatura at the end of episode 10, season 2, of *Westworld*.

A scene from the 1991 film *Grand Canyon*, with Steve Martin lying on a couch in a meeting room of the Ennis House during a therapy session with Mary McDonnell.

A scene from *Blade Runner* with Harrison Ford looking at a futuristic version of downtown Los Angeles from his apartment balcony in the Ennis House. The balcony and walls were likely a composite image, and the skyline was created with CGI.

Evan Rachel Wood touching a cross motif at Jeffrey Wright's future home.

many incised with Wright's distinctive cross motif. Bernard explains that he really looks forward to moving into this house with his sons when it's finished. Then Dolores walks up to one of the walls and runs her fingers slowly over one of the textile blocks, pausing them for a moment at the center of a cross. As they are leaving this construction site, she asks Bernard to let her visit the house after he moves in, and he promises to do so.

In the next scene, the story jumps ahead to when the Westworld hosts led by Dolores are killing all the humans around them. She explains to one of the other hosts why she wants to kill humans. "I used to see the beauty in this world. Now I see the truth!" Next, she has a flashback to the night she visited Bernard's house, and we see her again briefly visiting the construction site. As this scene ends, we see her remembering her comment that night, "Have you ever seen anything so full of splendor?" as she stands along the deck of Bernard's house looking out at the city lights.

In episode 10 of season two, titled "The Passenger," the last scene takes place in the now completed house Bernard was building for himself. As this scene opens, we see a new character, Charlotte Hale, walking through the back garden of the Millard House, with the guesthouse seen to her left, and up to the rear entrance. She's the executive director of the board overseeing Westworld. But this woman is a host replica of Charlotte, played by Tessa Thompson. Dolores Abernathy has transferred her consciousness into this host's body in order to escape from Westworld. The scene then

Scene from *Westworld*, with Evan Rachel Wood and Jeffrey Wright at the site of his future home, the Millard House.

cuts to Charlotte walking through the dining room and segues to Dolores Abernathy talking to Bernard after she had rebuilt her original host body and transferred her consciousness back into it. It was previously revealed that Bernard is actually a host created by Dr. Ford in the image of Arnold Weber, the co-founder of Westworld. As this scene unfolds, Arnold-cum-Bernard is in the basement workshop of the Millard House, while Dolores talks to him about her plans to continue her rebellion until all of the humans are dead. Arnold says he must stop her from carrying out such a drastic plan. She then leaves the house, and the scene shifts to Arnold walking through the living room of the guesthouse with the heavy concrete fireplace on the rear wall and then out into the garden and past the pond. As he walks through the garden, he hears Dolores's voice saying, "We each gave the other a beautiful gift. A choice." She then adds, "We are the authors of our own stories now." As the episode ends, Arnold goes up to the heavy oak door in the garden wall and then pauses for a moment next to the patterned textile blocks lining the doorway before exiting and closing the door behind him.

In season three, the Millard House is used as Arnold/Bernard's House for two more episodes: "The Absence of Field" and "The Mother of Exiles." Dolores Abernathy, Arnold Weber/Bernard Lowe, Dr. Ford and Charlotte Hale all visit the house at various times during these episodes. The Millard House does not appear in any episodes in season four, which was the final season of Westworld. The producers planned a fifth season, but it was canceled before shooting could begin.

The first season of *Westworld* remains, as of this writing, the most watched first season of any original HBO series. It received a Rotten Tomatoes score of 87 percent. That dropped to 73 percent by the third season, and average viewership had declined by 81 percent between the first and the fourth season. The increasing complexity of the plotlines and the ever-changing characters no doubt caused many viewers to lose interest in the show after the first two seasons. However, the first season won much critical acclaim. During the first season, *TV Guide*'s Tim Surette wrote that the show's "real treat will be the intelligent discussion of whether robots will eventually kill us all." The *San Francisco Chronicle*'s Dave Weigand commented, "*Westworld* isn't easy to understand at first, but you will be hooked nonetheless by unusually intelligent storytelling, powerful visuals, and exceptionally nuanced performances." And Robert Bianco of *USA Today* stated, "The reward, beyond the visual splendors you've come to expect from big-budget HBO productions, is a set of characters who grow ever more complex."

By the fourth season, many TV critics had negative opinions of the Westworld's growing complexity. CNN's Brian Lowry summed up such negative views when he observed that "the show has become increasingly incomprehensible, at least for anyone not willing to put in the work trying to remember all the assorted connections, further complicated by the fact that dying in *Westworld* is often not a permanent state of affairs amid the confusion about who's truly human and who actually isn't." Despite such criticism, during its four seasons, *Westworld* received fifty-four Prime Time Emmy Award nominations and won four of those awards.

Series Facts

Original Writers: Jonathan Nolan, Lisa Joy
Stars: Anthony Hopkins, Evan Rachel Wood, Ed Harris, Thandiwe Newton, Jeffrey Wright, Tessa Thompson
Production Company: HBO Entertainment and Warner Bros. Entertainment
Running Time of Episodes: 48 to 91 minutes
Season Budgets: Season One: $88 million; Season Two: $107 million; Season Three: $100 million; Season Four: $160 million

Star Trek: Deep Space Nine (1993–1999)

Star Trek: Deep Space Nine was a science fiction TV series set in outer space in the twenty-fourth century. The series ran for seven seasons, with 176 episodes. It was inspired by the success of its predecessor, *Star Trek: The Next Generation*, and was the first *Star Trek* series that did not involve the creator of the original series, Gene Roddenberry. It was also the first of this franchise to be set mostly on a space station and not a starship and to have a Black actor portray its main character: Starfleet Commander Benjamin Sisko, played by Avery Brooks. This TV series began after the first six *Star Trek* movies were released between 1979 and 1991 and was inspired by their popularity.

At the start of this series, Earth has joined the United Federation of Planets. The premise of the series revolves around the ongoing battle between two warring species, the Cardassians (not the ubiquitous Armenian American family famous for being famous) and the Bajorans, who have successfully rebelled against the imperialistic Cardassians, who had long occupied their planet, Bajor. Deep Space Nine is the new name for a space station near Bajor, which had been built during the occupation of that planet by the Cardassians. Commander Sisko has been assigned by the United Federation to oversee this space station.

The Millard House was used as a location for a scene in season two of *Star Trek: Deep Space Nine*, during the nineteenth episode, titled "Blood Oath." This episode aired on March 28, 1994, and drew nearly eight and a half million viewers. It focused on four main characters who attack the hideout of their old enemy the "Albino," which they plan to assault near the end of the episode. Three of these characters are warriors who first appeared in the original *Star Trek* series: the Klingons Kor, Koloth and Kang (nothing like a heavy dose of alliteration to spice up a TV series!). These three warriors are played by John Colicos, William Campbell and Michael Ansara, respectively. Fourth is the lead female character of the series Jadzia Dax, Commander Sisko's science officer, played by Terry Farrell. The three Klingons have sworn a blood oath to kill the Albino to get revenge for harming their families several decades ago, and Jadzia insists on joining them. All four transport down to the surface of the planet Bajor to carry out their mission. In the final scene, they appear in a jungle-like setting, within sight of the Albino's fortress, which is the Millard House. The lush tropical-like setting of the Millard House is well suited for an exotic location on another planet.

About thirty-four minutes into the episode, the north façade of the Millard House is visible on the left, while a CGI tower extension above the garden wall is visible on the right to make the site appear more like a fortress. About a minute later, Jadzia is shown sneaking into the rear garden through a gateway, then running past the guesthouse, which represents the Albino's blockhouse. Meanwhile the Klingon warriors are shown edging closer to the fortress as we see the upper walls and windows of the Millard House through the trees. A few seconds later, the rear façade of the guesthouse is seen as a series of explosions engineered by Jadzia blows out the door and windows (clearly a CGI effect). Then we see the Albino standing outside the blockhouse with the geometric patterns of the textile block walls clearly visible behind him. The remainder of this episode depicts the pitched battle between the Klingons and the Albino's forces inside the blockhouse, which is a set that bears no resemblance to the interior of the Millard House.

Critical response to the *Star Trek: Deep Space Nine* was mostly positive. *TV Guide* felt it was "the best acted, written, produced and altogether finest" Star Trek series. Another critic, Andrew Robinson, wrote in an online review, "It's not the most popular because it's the most morally ambiguous—Whenever you have characters who are grey rather than black and white—although they are more interesting, they are more difficult for people to get a handle on."

Scene from *Star Trek: Deep Space Nine*, with the Millard House on the left and a CGI of a fortress tower above.

The series did win praise from some Black and Latino viewers for the way it portrayed its minority characters, as well as having actors such as Alexander Siddig, who portrayed Dr. Bashir and is of North African heritage. *Star Trek: Deep Space Nine* was never as popular as its two predecessors, the original series and *Star Trek: The Next Generation.* But it earned a loyal following, as evidenced by the fact that it ran for seven seasons. It was nominated for thirty-one Emmy Awards, including costumes, special effects, art direction, make-up, cinematography and music. It won four Emmys; two for make-up, one for special effects and one for the main title music.

Series Facts

Original Writers: Rick Berman, Michael Piller
Production Company: Paramount Domestic Television
Stars: Avery Brooks, René Auberjonois, Terry Farrell, Alexander Siddig
Series Original Air Date: January 3, 1993
Running Time: 45 minutes
Series Budget: $1.1 million to $2 million per episode

6

HOME BASE OF THE VENTURE BROTHERS' NEMESIS

THE JOHN STORER HOUSE, 8161 HOLLYWOOD BOULEVARD, LOS ANGELES

Frank Lloyd Wright's residential architecture is usually associated with low-lying, ground-hugging shapes. The most readily recognizable feature of his houses is their horizontal massing and sweeping horizontal lines. Yet on a steep upslope lot in the Hollywood Hills, at the mouth of Laurel Canyon and just a few blocks from Sunset Boulevard, Wright designed a very vertical house in 1923 for John Storer, a homeopathic physician who had moved from Wisconsin to LA to establish a new practice in the booming Southern California economy. After failing his state medical board examination, Storer turned to selling real estate, at which he was quite successful. He hired Wright to design a home for him that would reflect his new financial status. The Storer House was later owned for several decades by the prolific Hollywood producer Joel Silver, and it was depicted in the 2003 to 2018 animated TV series *The Venture Brothers* (also styled *Bros.*).

The front façade of the three-level Storer House faces south and is dominated by a row of four two-story tall concrete pillars that draw the eye upward, from the entry-level concrete terrace to the flat roof. These pillars line a wall made of wood-framed latticed windows that reveal the living room and dining room on the upper levels. This creates a dramatic visual effect when seen from the curb, giving this home an impressive façade in a neighborhood of upscale houses. The Storer House is one of the four textile block houses Wright designed in Southern California and is another

South façade of the Storer House. *Photo by Joel Puliatti.*

example of his Mayan Temple style. The overall effect of this house is of a Pre-Columbian temple partially hidden among exotic jungle vegetation. Several mature eucalyptus trees tower above the house at the rear of the lot, and thick stands of bamboo line the driveway along the east side of the property. Wright's concept was to create the impression of the house being an extension of the landscape. However, when construction was completed in 1924, this part of the Hollywood Hills did not have the lush vegetation it has today, so it was many years before Wright's romantic vision would be realized. Wright's son Lloyd designed the landscaping and supervised the construction.

The Mayan design influence is reflected in the cutout cross motif incised into many of the concrete blocks that line the exterior and interior walls. This motif is similar to the one that Wright used on the Millard House but not a ubiquitous as it is at the Pasadena site. The living space has a total of 2,967 square feet in a T-shaped floor plan, with five bedrooms and three baths. The Storer House is approached via a curved driveway that leads to a one-car garage at the east end of the home. The main entrance is set into the wall of two-story windows along the south façade. The front door is near the west end of the concrete terrace running along the south side of the house. Wright placed a shallow pool with a small fountain in the middle of this terrace, enhancing the romantic effect of the setting. The wall of windows admits lots of natural light in the morning, thus bathing the rooms on the south side in the abundant sunlight that is so common in Southern California.

The front door leads directly into the formal dining room. Between the dining room and the living room upstairs, the contrast of the ceiling heights creates a strong impression on first-time visitors. Here Wright was employing of one of his favorite techniques of compression and release. The ceiling of the dining room is fairly low, with elegant polished redwood paneling and open beams. The north wall has the same tall, latticed windows as the south side, with a door that opens onto a secluded concrete terrace surrounded by trees and shrubs. There is a long, narrow swimming pool in the middle of this terrace where Wright's original plans called for a sunken garden. Adjacent to the dining room is a small kitchen designed by Eric Wright, Frank's grandson, during a 1980s restoration. There is also a bedroom and full bath in this wing. At the west end of the dining room is a freestanding fireplace and flue faced in concrete blocks. Wright created a cozy nook in front of this fireplace, with built-in bookshelves lining the staircase that leads to the upper-level rooms. The floor of the dining room is made of textured concrete in eighteen-inch-square panels. Some of the wall sconces in the dining room and upper levels are original Wright designs.

The main staircase along the west end of the house is made of concrete and has wide landings that provide views of the dining room and the living room on the third level. On the second level halfway up the staircase, Wright placed two spacious bedrooms, with a full bath between them. The stairs continue up to the grand living room, which is truly magnificent in both its scale and design features. The ceilings here are sixteen feet tall, with the same polished redwood paneling and open beaming as the dining room. The wood latticed windows here, however, have leaded geometric patterns across the top. In the northwest corner, Wright placed a concrete fireplace with a wide hearth and a flue decorated with quoining patterns

Living room and sun terrace of the Storer House. *Photo by Joel Puliatti.*

along the corners and front. The windows lining the north wall look out over the rear terrace. Wright designed a passageway between the back of the fireplace and these windows so that one would emerge into the tall space of the living room in a most impressive way. He also designed a raised landing on the west wall that overlooks the entire living room. This landing opens onto a large concrete roof deck, similar to the deck he placed on the roof of the Millard House. The floors of the living room are made of rich, warm oak.

One of the most pleasing features of the Storer House is a long, spacious private deck, or sun terrace, that Wright designed off the east end of the living room, above the garage. The terrace is shaded by rows of blue and yellow fabric panels lining a metal canopy, a full sixteen feet above the concrete floors. This terrace is a recent restoration of Wright's original design. Its colorful canopy creates a cheerful space for al fresco dining, reading or relaxing, all activities that the warm climate of Los Angeles provides ample opportunities to enjoy.

John Storer did not live in this house for very long; he sold it in 1927. The wife of the architect Rudolph Schindler rented it for a while after that. The house passed through several owners during the next few decades. In 1984, the noted Hollywood producer Joel Silver bought the house and immediately began a full restoration of the residence and grounds to correct the effects of years of deferred maintenance. This was done under the supervision of Eric Wright and Martin Weil, former president of the Los Angeles Conservancy, which was also involved in the restoration of Wright's Ennis House. During this restoration, many of the concrete blocks were replaced with new ones made from soil from the backyard mixed with concrete, thus remaining loyal to Wright's original concept of this house as an extension of the landscape. When the restoration work was done, the *New York Times* declared that the Storer House "is widely considered the best-preserved Wright building in Los Angeles." After spending "a small fortune" on the restoration, Silver put the house up for sale in 2001. It was first listed for $3.5 million. But given its relatively small size in comparison with other more recently built houses in the vicinity, Silver had trouble attracting a buyer. The house finally sold for $2.9 million in 2002. The house was listed for sale again in 2013 and sold for $6.8 million in 2015. The John Storer House was added to the National Register of Historic Places in 1971, and it was designated as a Los Angeles Historic-Cultural Monument in 1972.

Joel Silver's Film Production Company Logo

A textile block at the Storer House. This design was used as a logo for Joel Silver's film production company. *Photo by Joel Puliatti.*

Joel Silver has been one of the most prolific and successful producers of American films over the past several decades. His production company, Silver Pictures, was founded in 1980. It created such iconic film series as *Die Hard*, *Lethal Weapon* and *The Matrix*. From 1991 through 2005, an image of one of the textile blocks from the Storer House, with its Mayan geometric patterns, was used as the logo for his film production company. This logo appeared at the end of some of his company's most popular films: the *Matrix* trilogy, *Conspiracy Theory*, *Swordfish*, *Cradle 2 the Grave*, and *Romeo Must Die*. This was during the period when Silver was carrying out his meticulous restoration of the Storer House and was evidence of the producer's well-known admiration for Frank Lloyd Wright's work.

The Venture Brothers (2003–2018)

The Venture Brothers was an animated adult action TV series that ran for seven seasons between its pilot in 2003 and final episode in 2018. There were eighty-one episodes of twenty-two minutes each and four specials during that time. The premise, to quote IMDb, is, "the warped misadventures of a boy adventurer turned washed up middle-aged mad scientist, Dr. Rusty Venture, and his moronic sons and their maniac bodyguard, and his arch nemesis, incompetent supervillain The Monarch and his masculine sounding paramour, Dr. Girlfriend." During the series, Monarch and Dr. Girlfriend move into a new house in a community called "Malice." The style and features of their home are based on the Storer House. After they move into this house, The Monarch and Dr. Girlfriend are shown standing at the front window, with the room behind them resembling the living room of the Storer House. This is clear evidence that Frank Lloyd Wright's influence on Hollywood had extended to the design of graphic TV productions by the early twenty-first century.

7

A DYSTOPIAN DESERT SETTING IN THE HILLS ABOVE MALIBU

ARCH OBOLER COMPOUND, 32436 MULHOLLAND HIGHWAY, MALIBU

The Santa Monica Mountains rise steeply from the Pacific Coast Highway above Malibu, reaching heights of over 2,200 feet at their highest peaks. These rugged, craggy slopes have, as of yet, remained unspoiled, with only a handful of modern McMansions sprinkled among the few older ranch houses and historic homes that were built before the 1950s. In this arid, semi-desert setting, Frank Lloyd Wright designed a "desert compound," the Arch Oboler Gatehouse and Retreat, between 1940 and 1955. An early dystopian feature film, the 1951 movie *Five*, about the aftermath of a nuclear war, was filmed partially at this compound. Sadly, the Oboler Compound was totally gutted by the Woolsey Fire in 2018, which was a portent of the much greater damage caused by the Pacific Palisades Fire in January 2025. Efforts are underway by the Frank Lloyd Wright Conservancy to restore the compound using Wright's surviving plans.

The setting of the Oboler Compound is one of the most spectacular of any of Wright's residential designs. This site is a 107-acre tract in an unincorporated section of Los Angeles County, where the landscape spreads out across a range of rocky peaks and crags, with valleys and level areas in between. The elevation of this site varies from 2,000 to 2,200 feet above sea level. The views from every part of this tract are magnificent, especially at sunset, with the steep slopes of the mountains cascading down toward the Pacific Ocean in the distance, when the bright California sun fills the sky with reds, pinks and purples on a clear day.

Arch Oboler was a Hollywood producer, director and screenwriter who also wrote plays and scripts for radio, including the 1930s program *Lights Out*, and a series of plays for NBC. His radio plays starred an impressive array of A-list Hollywood actors, including Jimmy Stewart, James Cagney, Edward G. Robinson and Bette Davis. Oboler met Wright when he was hired to provide film projectors for Wright's private movie theater at his Taliesin West studio in Arizona. When Oboler decided he wanted to build a residence and retreat in the Santa Monica Mountains, one that would include post-production facilities and a writing studio, he asked Wright to design it for him. Wright's son Lloyd found the perfect site, and after purchasing it, Oboler commissioned Wright to design a gatehouse, a retreat/guesthouse, a residence, stables, an office and children's playrooms. The gatehouse was completed in 1940, the retreat in 1941 and the additions to the gatehouse were built between 1944 and 1955, but the main residence was never constructed. Oboler's mercurial finances, which rose and fell with his various film ventures, kept him from being able to afford the cost of the primary residence that Wright had designed for him. Oboler gave this compound the fittingly romantic name of Eagle Feather, and he named the studio perched above the western edge of the site after his wife, calling it Eleanor's Retreat.

Frank Lloyd Wright's love of desert settings was well established by the time he got the commission to design the Oboler Compound. Wright had moved most of his practice from his original studio, Taliesin East in Wisconsin, to Arizona in 1937, where he designed Taliesin West near Scottsdale, which remained his headquarters until his death in 1959. There, he developed a highly personal genre of design he called "desert aesthetic," to designate architecture suited to arid climates like Arizona and Southern California. He used local stone set into concrete for masonry walls that made them appear to have grown right out of the desert terrain. He also used wood siding on upper walls and low-angled or flat roofs with wide overhanging eaves that made buildings seem to nestle comfortably into the landscape. Wright used this design system on several homes in the Western United States during his later career, from the Rose Pauson House in Phoenix, Arizona, in 1939 to the Berger House in San Anselmo, California, in 1950. The Oboler Compound displays all of these characteristics, especially when viewed from the craggy peaks that surround it, where it seems to be an extension of the desert environment. Wright's use of rubblestone pillars interspersed with plate-glass doors and windows creates a strong rhythmic quality, as does the outward tapering of the upper walls. One concession to the limitations of this system was the replacing of the original redwood siding with cedar clapboards when the redwood boards cracked in the dry climate.

The approach to the Oboler Compound is down a long, level driveway lined with walls made from fieldstone (or as Wright called it, "rubblestone") in a variety of textures and colors taken from the site. This was the same material Wright used on most of the exterior walls for the rest of the compound. At the end of the driveway, on the right, is the gatehouse, which is actually one wing of a T-shaped group of structures all under one roof. The gatehouse itself runs east to west, and its long northern wall has a row of stone pillars that rise about two feet above the roofline, creating the impression of an ancient Middle Eastern fortress or of the battlements of a medieval castle on a mountaintop. The gatehouse wing was the Oboler's living quarters, which had a small living room, with an open kitchen on the

Living room of the main residence at the Oboler Compound. *Photo by Joel Puliatti.*

north end. This space had a warm, intimate feel, with a fireplace faced with rubblestone on the east wall, a cedar plank ceiling that tapers upward toward the middle and recessed lighting in the kitchen lined with cutout geometric patterns in wood. To the left of the kitchen was a bedroom and a full bath. From the living room, there was a superb view of the Pacific Ocean on clear days. The couple who owned the compound when I was there in 2013 described this pleasant living space as "a small work of art—a gem."

The children's wing had an open staircase (later enclosed), which led to a children's theater and playroom downstairs. This wing had two levels, with the first level partially set into the gentle upsloping hillside on which it was sited. A rubblestone fireplace was set into the west wall on both levels, and steel-framed glass doors on the south end opened onto a terrace on the ground level. On the upper level, steel-framed picture windows across the upper wall provided a lovely view of a man-made pond that was part of the original landscape design by Lloyd Wright. The ceilings in this wing were similar to those in the gatehouse, with coffered cedar planks and geometric cutout patterns on the recessed lighting. There were two bedrooms and two baths on the upper level of the children's wing. The theater and playroom were used as a family entertainment center by the Obolers and often provided amusement for Eleanor and her four sons while Arch worked on his film projects. The third wing of the gatehouse ran east to west from the carport. This was the stable wing, which at times was also used as a workspace for Arch. It has a kitchen and an office, as well as a laundry room, bedroom, full bath and sitting area.

The most impressive edifice in the Oboler Compound was Eleanor's Retreat. This was a small separate structure that crowned the top of a craggy outcrop of rock near the southeast corner of the property. Wright designed it to be a self-contained unit that could be used as a guesthouse or as a workplace or retreat for Eleanor. The main space was a light-filled open room with panoramic views of the Santa Monica Mountains from picture windows on the east, south and west sides. A wide, open-hearth fireplace composed of rubblestone and concrete dominated the north side of this room, with a full bath behind it. The floors were made from rubblestone, and two narrow windows on the west wall flank the fireplace, with a built-in desk below one window and built-in shelves in the corners and along the walls. In his typical fashion, Wright gave the retreat a flat roof, with wide overhanging eaves that helped shade the interior when the Southern California sun is at its most intense. All of these features were utilized to good effect throughout the film *Five*.

Eleanor's Retreat at the Oboler Compound. *Photo by Joel Puliatti.*

The outer walls of the retreat were sheathed in cedar planks, with rubblestone used for the lower sections of the exterior, as well as the stairs and retaining wall leading up to the doorway and the terrace running along the north and south sides. Wright's apprentice John Lautner oversaw the construction of the Oboler Compound. Wright came to inspect the site in 1941, when Eleanor's retreat was finished. He was unhappy with the way Lautner had situated the stairs. So, Wright had some of the "boys" from his staff at Taliesin West rebuild the stairs and retaining wall to run north to south, in a straight line along the hillside.

Arch and Eleanor Oboler lived in their compound for over four decades. During those years, Arch worked on several small budget Hollywood films, including directing, writing and producing the first feature-length 3-D movie in color, called *Bwana Devil,* which was released in 1952. He also wrote, directed and produced the 1951 science fiction film *Five,* which was shot in and around the compound. Arch died in 1987, and Eleanor lived on the property for a few more years. After she moved out of the compound in the early 1990s, the property was put on the market, and there was a contingent sale to a developer with plans to demolish the compound and divide the property into fifteen lots for luxury homes. He withdrew his offer when the housing market crashed in the early '90s. In 1996, Dorothy and John Knight bought the Oboler Compound and began a major restoration of the buildings and grounds, including repairing the damage to the structures from years of neglected maintenance and installing a large pool just below Eleanor's Retreat. They completed their restoration in 2017, one year before the Woolsey Fire swept through the site and destroyed all of the

View of the Santa Monica Mountains from Eleanor's Retreat. *Photo by Joel Puliatti.*

structures but left most of the "desert masonry" used for the foundations and walls intact.

The local government agencies that oversee restoration of properties damaged by fire at first told the owners they would have to demolish the remaining sections of all the structures as a "safety measure" and in order to remove any environmental hazards. However, the Frank Lloyd Wright Revival Initiative contacted Wright's grandson Eric and other leading architects and scholars of Wright's work, who were able to convince these authorities to leave all of the remaining masonry in place, to be incorporated into a full restoration of the compound in the future. As of this writing, the Frank Lloyd Wright Revival Initiative is organizing an effort to raise the millions of dollars it will take to rebuild this irreplaceable portion of Frank Lloyd Wright's innovative "desert aesthetic" design system.

Five (1951)

This black-and-white feature film was one of the first dystopian movies by a Hollywood producer and the first feature film to depict the aftermath of a nuclear war. The theme of a handful of survivors of an atomic war struggling to stay alive and sane in a barren setting was quite timely for American audiences in the year it was released. The Cold War with the Soviet Union and China, which had recently become a communist dictatorship, had become a limited hot war after the start of the Korean War in 1950. There was even serious talk among some high-ranking U.S. military officials and politicians of using atomic bombs on the battlefield in Korea to gain the upper hand against the Chinese army units that had entered the war to aid their North Korean allies, as they had pushed the American military back down the peninsula in the winter of 1950–51. There was heated discussion in the U.S. media of the possibility of the Soviet Union entering the war and using their nuclear arsenal if the United States deployed its atomic weapons, thus sparking another world war with far deadlier consequences that the last one.

The *Five* who are the only survivors of a worldwide nuclear war are a disparate group of adults: Roseanne Rogers, a pregnant woman; Michael Rogin, a young poet and philosopher; Charles, a Black man; Eric, a mountain climber who was on Mount Everest when the nuclear war broke out; and Mr. Barnstaple, a wealthy banker. Oboler chose not to give all of his characters both first and last names, probably because these five people each symbolize a distinct aspect of American culture during that time. Michael represents the passions and idealism of youth, Charles represents the oppression of minorities in the United State, Mr. Barnstaple represents greed and self-absorption, Eric represents arrogance and fascism and Roseanne represents all women of child-bearing age. These five all eventually end up at the Oboler Compound.

The movie begins with images of nuclear bombs exploding all over the world (obtained from tests filmed by the U.S. military). Then the words "A Story About The Day After Tomorrow" appear on the screen, followed by a biblical quote: "A deadly wind passeth over it, —and it is gone." Next, several world landmarks are shown with smoke swirling around them: Parliament and the Tower Bridge in London; Russian Orthodox churches inside the Kremlin walls; the Eiffel Tower; the Taj Mahal; New York skyscrapers; and finally, the San Francisco skyline and Golden Gate Bridge. Then the scene switches to a bird's-eye view of the Santa Monica Mountains as the camera sweeps over them to a narrow country road. A young woman is seen stumbling along this road, clearly lost and desperate. This is Roseanne Rogers, played by Susan Douglas Rubes. Then the view switches to eye level as she finds an abandoned car and pulls the driver's door open to find a skeleton behind the wheel. Next, we see Roseanne rushing through the main street of a small town empty of people, where she sees a headline in a shop window that reads "World Annihilation Feared by Scientists." She begins crying out, "Somebody help me, *please!*" over and over as she passes skeletons inside cars and lying in doorways.

Six minutes into the film, we get our first glimpse of the Oboler Compound as Roseanne climbs up a hillside toward a small wood and stone structure perched on the crest of the hill. This is Eleanor's Retreat, which is the focus of the rest of the movie and the only structure in the compound shown in *Five* (the additions to the gatehouse were still under construction at that time). Oboler chose this building as the main setting for this film because its isolation as a self-contained unit overlooking the arid mountain setting was symbolic of the isolation that the five survivors endure as they try to build a new world. As Roseanne reaches the base of the retreat, the desert masonry along its foundation is clearly seen, as well as on the stairway as she stumbles up to the door and goes inside. A fire is going in the rubblestone fireplace. We see cookware on a table and books lining the built-in bookshelves along the wall, but no one else is there. Suddenly, the door opens, and a young bearded man walks in. This

Scene from *Five*, with Susan Douglas Rubes on the steps to Eleanor's Retreat.

is Michael Rogin, played by William Phipps. Roseanne is startled by his sudden entrance and faints to the floor.

In the next scene, the two of them are sitting outside on the small deck that's part of the terrace along the exterior of the retreat. Michael tells her he has an "MA in English Lit," but he could only get a job as a guide at the Empire State Building, which is where he was when the bombs began to fall. He was on the top floor of the building and the only person there who survived. So, he spent the next several weeks making his way across the country to the West Coast. She doesn't speak to him yet, and he goes off hunting in the hills. When he returns, he takes her inside, and Roseanne finally tells him she was at a hospital in an X-ray room when the explosions began. Michael says that the lead-lined walls probably protected her from the radiation. She asks him if he thinks anyone else might be alive, since she was separated from her husband when the war started and still wants to find him. Michael tells her he saw no one alive in the cities he passed through on his journey west. Then he tells Roseanne to forget her husband. "He's dead, they're all dead! We live in a dead world! And I'm glad it's dead—cheap honky-tonk of a world."

That night, they are seen sitting by the fireplace and then walking over to the wide picture window and looking out at the moonlit landscape. Michael suddenly grabs her and tries to kiss her, saying, "We're all alone, there's only us left!" She pushes him away, telling him that she's pregnant with her husband's baby and still hopes to find him alive. The next morning, they are outside again, with the cedar clapboards along the upper walls behind them. She asks him to take her "to the city" to see if her husband is still alive. He agrees, but they are interrupted by the sound of a car horn blaring. They rush to the road to find two men sitting in a jeep. They are an old white man, Mr. Barnstaple, played by Earl Lee, and a young Black man, Charles, played by Charles Lampkin. Barnstaple says they were locked in a time release vault at the bank where he was president when the bombing began. When the time release opened the door, they went outside and found an abandoned jeep. So, they decided to drive up the coast to see if anyone else was still alive. Michael and Roseanne invite them to stay for a while at the retreat, since they must be tired and hungry by now, and there are plenty of canned goods for them to eat.

The next day, as the four of them sit outside the retreat, Mr. Barnstaple notices bruising on his arms and thinks it might be from radiation poisoning. Later he tells Roseanne he wants to go to the ocean to see it again. The other three put him in the jeep, and they drive down to the beach. While Barnstaple talks as he lays dying about how he wanted to go to sea when he was young but gave up his dream to become a banker

Susan Douglas Rubes on the dessert masonry deck of Eleanor's Retreat in *Five*.

One of the four male survivors in *Five* inside Eleanor's Retreat.

and make money, the others notice a body in the surf wash up on the beach. They run over to find it's a middle-aged man who's still alive. This is Eric, played by James Anderson. Eric explains he crossed the ocean by boat and plane after reaching the summit of Mount Everest (this was two years before the first recorded accomplishment of that feat by Sir Edmund Hillary and Tenzing Norgay). Back at the retreat, tensions soon develop between Eric and the others, as his racist attitudes and arrogance are revealed. The rest of the movie focuses on the escalating conflict caused by Eric's antagonism toward Michael and Charles and how Roseanne is caught in the middle of their rivalry as the birth of her baby nears. One of the other firsts for this film occurs during the later part of the story, when Charles greets a new day by reciting a poem called "The Creation" by noted Black poet James Weldon Johnson. This was very likely the first time white audiences in America heard a poem by a Black writer in a feature film from a mainstream producer.

After it was completed, Oboler sold *Five* to Columbia Pictures to distribute for much more than it cost to produce. Audience reception to the film was lukewarm, probably due to the disconcerting theme and dark mood of the story. The response of critics was mixed. The *New York Times* critic Bosley

Crowther said about the characters, "Mr. Oboler has imagined so little of significance for them to do—that there is nothing to be learned from watching them." However, some of the most famous American critics felt differently. Hedda Hopper said "*Five* is shocking," Louella Parsons called it "amazing" and Walter Winchell said it was "dynamic." And a 2015 review by Sean Axmaker on Turner Classic Movies stated, "For all its budgetary limitations, it's a strikingly atmospheric and handsome film, and Oboler creates an eerie sense of isolation with simple techniques."

Film Facts

Director: Arch Oboler
Studio: Columbia Pictures
Release Date: April 25, 1951
Stars: William Phipps, Susan Douglas Rubes, James Anderson, Charles Lampkin
Running Time: 91 minutes
Budget: $75,000
Box Office Gross: not documented

8

FRANK LLOYD WRIGHT DESIGNED OUR HOUSE—OOPS!

CLINTON WALKER HOUSE, SCENIC ROAD AT MARTIN STREET, CARMEL

The Clinton Walker House is one of Frank Lloyd Wright's most popular residences with the general public, having appeared in many books about Wright's work, and is admired by the many tourists who stroll past it every day along the shoreline of Carmel Bay. It was also one of Wright's favorite residential designs, one that he referred to as a "little masterpiece" that was perfectly suited to its unique setting. Also, it is featured in the 1959 Hollywood blockbuster movie *A Summer Place* (or was it?). The story of how this house was created and how it (sort of) appeared in a major feature film is a quite a colorful tale.

In 1945, Clinton Walker's widow, Della Brooks Walker, purchased a one-acre lot on a prominent outcropping along Carmel Bay. She wrote a letter to Frank Lloyd Wright on June 13, 1945, that described her site and asked if he would design a beachfront house for her. Her vivid description of the setting intrigued Wright.

"I own a rocky point of land in Carmel, California, extending into the Pacific Ocean. The surface is flat, and it is located at the end of a white sand beach. I am a woman living alone. I wish protection from the wind and privacy from the road and a house as enduring as the rocks, but as transparent and charming as the waves and as delicate as a seashore. You are the only man who can do this. Will you help me?"

Before she decided to write this letter, Della Walker told her friends and family that the reason she wanted Wright to be her architect was because of his design of Fallingwater. "If he could do that for a stream," her great-grandson quoted her as saying, "just imagine what he could do with an ocean?" Obviously, Della Walker was a woman who knew exactly what she wanted and knew how to express herself eloquently enough to get it. As Wright was to find out to his chagrin during their working relationship, she was not just an eager admirer who would bend to Wright's domineering personality but also one of his strong-minded female clients who insisted on getting her way and wouldn't take no for an answer, much like Aline Barnsdall.

When Wright received Walker's letter, he responded promptly, saying he would be happy to design her house. Wright's work on other buildings delayed the start of work on this project. Construction finally began in April 1948, but a shortage of building materials during the Korean War interrupted the project once again. The house was finally completed in November 1952. Walker lived there alone for twenty-six years, until her death in 1978.

The Walker House is a single-story, five-room residence with 1,200 square feet of living space, three bedrooms, a combination living room/dining room, three bathrooms and a small kitchen. The back bedroom was enlarged in the

The Walker House, which Wright called "the cabin on the rocks." *Photo by Joel Puliatti.*

early 1960s from drawings done by Wright and executed by Sandy Walker, Della's grandson. This is not a typical Usonian house but a unique example of Wright's design philosophy, a gem he created to fit perfectly into its natural setting through integrating the structure and materials with its site. The fact that it was one of Wright's favorite commissions out of all his West Coast work is clearly indicated in his correspondence with Della Walker, both during and after its construction, in which he referred affectionately to the house as the "Cabin on the Rocks."

The living room/dining room faces due west and is the most impressive room in the house, with its sweeping view of Carmel Bay, the white sand beaches that line it and the blue waters of the Pacific Ocean beyond. The tiers of metal-framed windows that encircle this room are slanted outward, to reduce the glare from the sunlight on the water in the late afternoon. The wide overhanging eaves of the low-hipped roof also serve to reduce glare. The roof was originally clad in blue-green porcelain to mirror the colors of the ocean. However, as with so many other Wright houses, this roof began leaking soon after construction was completed, so it was replaced with a copper-clad roof about 1960. The living room was shaped in a four-by-four-foot parallelogram pattern, which was used for the entire floor plan.

The most distinctive feature of the Walker House is the west end, which forms a prow-like projection, as does the terrace that runs around the front of the living room, which is made from concrete faced with Carmel stone. These prominent prow-shaped features, pointing out to sea, create the impression of a ship about to be launched into the ocean. Wright placed a row of window seats all around the living room, to make it easier for residents and visitors to enjoy the view. He also designed a small dining table for this room, composed of triangular sections, and designed a set of chairs for it. The open-hearth fireplace that forms the rear wall of the living room is faced with Carmel stone. When it was first installed, the stones were set incorrectly in a horizontal pattern. So, Aaron Green, Wright's supervising architect, told the contractors to take them out and reinstall them in an upward slant as Wright had intended. The living room ceiling tilts upward from the edges toward the center and was made from combed plywood. The walls throughout the house were made from cedar panels with beveled battens, and the floors are made of concrete slabs, scored in a four-by-four parallelogram pattern and stained Wright's favorite Cherokee red.

A gallery-style hallway runs along the south side of the house, which is sheltered from the glare of the afternoon sun by custom-designed blinds, with slats that tilt at just the correct angle to allow views of the beach and still

Kitchen of the Walker House with "Della's door." *Photo by Joel Puliatti.*

provide shade. The small front door is at the west end of the hallway, and two bedrooms and two baths open onto this hallway. The enlarged master suite in the rear wing has a large adjoining bath and a wide fireplace along the north wall lined in Carmel stone. This bedroom opens onto a spacious, trapezoidal deck along the north side of the house that has unobstructed views of the beach and the ocean below. The overall effect of the interior of the Walker House is that of a cozy, yet comfortable and inviting space that makes visitors want to stay for a long time.

Before construction on the Walker House was completed, a request from Della Walker about the kitchen caused a battle royal with Wright. She wanted a door put into the north wall of the kitchen so she could put the trash out easily. In a testy letter written on February 27, 1951, Wright stated his strenuous objection.

"Again we are up in the air—Looks very much like the Cabin on the Rocks was on the rocks in more than one sense. You were once of my mind about the cabin. You gave me reason to think so, and I was happy to build it as I put my best mind and heart into producing a little masterpiece appropriate to the unique site. An ordinary 'door and window' house on that site would look as foolish as a hen resting where you ought to see a seagull. I am unwilling to spoil my charming seabird and substitute a hen. You don't need me for that. Anyone can do it."

Wright and Walker arrived at a compromise—to sink the trash can into a hole in the concrete deck so it couldn't be seen by passersby, thus removing one of Wright's concerns. He still opposed putting the door in the kitchen wall, but since *she* was paying the contractors, Della got her door, exactly where she wanted it, thus having the rare satisfaction of getting the famed Wright to change his original plans to meet his client's needs.

There was another testy exchange between Walker and Wright when the construction was nearing completion. Della hired the renowned landscape architect Thomas Church to design the landscape scheme for the exterior of her house. When some of Wright's staff informed him of this, Wright again fired off an indignant letter of protest dated March 21, 1952.

"Distressing news from several quarters. One of my former apprentices says to Aaron Green 'Someone has ruined Mr. Wright's house with landscaping.' Walter Olds, distressed, said 'Mrs. Walker has hired a professional landscaper to undue [*sic*] all Mr. Wright has done for her'. If you did hire one, it is the first time it has happened to me in a long lifetime of building. The first destructive insult. I don't believe it."

Walker House, south façade. *Photo by Joel Puliatti.*

"Throughout the nation, these destructive vermin plant a skirt of shrubbery around a house and stick up a couple of trees at the entrance. A 'William Worse than Wurster' might be benefitted by this stock performance. Not so the Cabin on the Rocks. Is it all true? —I hope what I hear is not true and loves labor lost. I love the Cabin and had it in my heart as well as my head."

But Walker stuck to her guns, and once again her desires prevailed over the heated objections of Wright. Thomas Church's landscape design was carried out largely as he had planned it, with no discernable detriment to the aesthetic effect of Wright's creation. In 2023, the Walker House was sold for the first time, to a new private owner, for $22 million, a record for a single-family residence in Monterey County. Anyone who has strolled along the white sand beaches of Carmel Bay and looked up to see the Walker House set so perfectly into its rocky outcropping would agree that the Cabin on the Rocks is indeed a little masterpiece that fits beautifully into its unique site.

A SUMMER PLACE (1959)

The theme song from the movie was everywhere in the months after the film was released. You couldn't escape it. Its lilting melody was heard in shopping malls, hotel lobbies, restaurants and even elevators. It was the number one song on Billboard's pop chart for nine weeks, and it stayed in the top forty for more than four months. The popularity of the theme from *A Summer Place* was largely due to the success of the film itself. The movie was based on the controversial best-selling 1958 novel of the same title by Sloan Wilson. It also generated its own controversy because of the risqué topics it depicted, which had rarely been dealt with so forthrightly in a major American film; premarital sex, adultery, a virginity exam, gender identity and alcoholism.

The story supposedly takes place on the East Coast, though in reality most of the scenes were filmed in California's Monterey County. The film begins with an unhappily married couple aboard a yacht arriving at a vacation resort on an island off the coast of Maine. They are Ken Jorgenson, played by Richard Egan, and his wife, Helen, played by Constance Ford, and with them is their teenage daughter Molly, played by Sandra Dee. Ken used to work as a lifeguard at this vacation home when he was a teenager twenty years ago and had a summer romance with the woman who is now the owner's wife, Sylvia Hunter, played by Dorothy McGuire. Her husband, Bart, played by Arthur Kennedy, comes from a wealthy family, and they also have an unhappy marriage, leading Bart to become a hopeless alcoholic and let their house become dilapidated. They have a teenage son, Johnny, played by Troy Donahue. In contrast to Bart's downward spiral, Ken has become a successful businessman, and Helen suspects he just wants to return to the island to flaunt his success to his former employer.

On board their yacht before they disembark, Ken and Helen have an argument over how Molly is dressed. Helen tells her daughter her outfit is too suggestive, especially when there's a teenage boy in the house where they'll be staying. Molly complains that the outfit her mother wants her wear makes her "look like a boy." Her father takes Molly's side, accusing his wife of wanting to suppress her daughter's sexuality and make her feel "sexless." This foreshadows the conflicts to come during their visit, when Helen vehemently expresses her distaste for any display of physical intimacy between her and Ken that night in their guest bedroom. This makes Ken nostalgic for the passion he once shared with Sylvia, and in the first few scenes where they are together, it's clear that they still have romantic feelings for each other, and they eventually express their desires and renew their love when they are alone in a shed on the grounds.

Meanwhile, Molly and Johnny are immediately attracted to each other when they meet. They take a walk around the grounds one night, the first time they are alone together, and end up kissing passionately before they're interrupted by Helen, who comes looking for Molly. Later, the two teenage lovers take a sailboat out on the bay, with Ken's permission, while he's away on business. But they get caught in rough weather that causes their boat to capsize, forcing them to spend the night on a beach. Helen calls the Coast Guard to search for them, and when they are found safe the next morning and brought back to the resort, she accuses them of having sex on the beach. They forcefully deny this, but Helen refuses to believe them, and she calls a doctor to the house to examine her daughter to see if she had sex with Johnny or is still a virgin. This sends Molly into emotional meltdown at being humiliated in front of a stranger. The exam proves that Molly is still a virgin, but feeling resentful of her mother, she runs away, which causes Johnny to threaten to kill Helen if she ever hurts Molly again.

Helen decides to summon the police this time to search for Molly and prevent her from ruining her life by continuing her romance with Johnny and to file a complaint against him for his threat to her. In the meantime, Ken has returned and angrily castigates Helen for the way she has treated their daughter. Helen responds with a fit of anger, and in front of Bart, Sylvia, Ken and Johnny, she reveals that she knows about Ken and Sylvia's renewed romance. This eventually leads to the acrimonious divorce of both couples and causes Molly and Johnny to become angry at Ken and Sylvia

Scene from *A Summer Place* as Dorothy McGuire and Sandra Dee enter the Walker House.

Dorothy McGuire and Sandra Dee in the "downstairs" of the Walker House in *A Summer Place*. This was a set; the real house is only one story.

for their illicit affair and breaking up their families. The teenagers are sent away in the fall to boarding schools hundreds of miles apart from each other. They remain in touch with phone calls and draw on each other for emotional support to get through their painful separation. Meanwhile, Ken and Sylvia get married but are saddened that their children refuse to attend the ceremony.

About an hour and a half into the movie, we see the Walker House, which is supposedly a beach house on the coast of Maine. In a previous scene, Ken had invited Molly and Johnny to visit the newlyweds in their new home during spring break. Molly arrives first, and we see the north side of the Walker House as a car drives toward it and then down the long driveway. As Sylvia walks with Molly up to the front entrance, she says proudly, "Frank Lloyd Wright designed our house!" But when she opens the front door, the interior does not resemble the real inside of the actual house. The living room is similar in style to Wright's design, but there is a wooden staircase at the left end of the room that leads "downstairs" to the guest bedrooms where Molly and Johnny will stay during their visit. This was almost certainly a set on a sound stage to make the house look like it had two stories and to control the lighting, to avoid the effect of the bright sunlight from the beach and make it easier to shoot the subsequent nighttime scenes. When Johnny arrives later on, we see the roof and prow of the Walker House shot from above. In an earlier scene the teenagers had tried to get a justice of the peace to marry them but are told they weren't of "legal age" to marry. So, Molly is still a virgin when the couple is reunited at the beach house.

During their visit, the teenagers avoid Ken and Sylvia, spending time on the beach alone together, where Johnny expresses his frustration at their not having had sex yet. One night, they tell the adults they are going to town to see the movie *King Kong*, as an excuse to be alone. In later scenes during the remainder of their visit, the other interior views of the beach house are also done on a set, with different décor and backgrounds than the real Walker House has. But the set designers for *A Summer Place* had clearly studied Wright's style and residences, unlike the set designers on *The Fountainhead*. Some of the details of the interior scenes incorporate Wright-like materials and features, such as Carmel stone facing, wide metal-framed picture glass windows and concrete fireplaces. At the end of Molly and Johnny's visit, their parents are seen standing on the prow-like deck at the front of the house as their kids walk back from the beach one more time. In the last scene of the film, Sylvia says to the teenagers on a subsequent visit, "We live in a glass house—we aren't throwing any stones."

A Summer Place was a hit after it was released, with large audiences going to see it in theaters across the country. However, even though its portrayal of sexual behavior seems tame by today's standards, it did raise objections from some viewers. There were reports of some parents taking their families out of the theater after the first references to premarital sex in the early scenes.

Troy Donahue leaving the Walker House in *A Summer Place*.

Reviews from critics were mixed. A review in one newsletter for independent theater owners before the release date praised the film, saying it would be "money in the bank at the box office" and that it was "a well-made bit of entertainment." But this reviewer went on to caution theater owners that the movie was "devoted almost exclusively to the most popular cinema topic of the day—sex." The *New York Times*' Harold Thompson wrote a review typical of the objections some people had to the film's overt themes of sexual morality, calling it "one of the most laboriously and garishly sex-scented movies in years." Although the total box office receipts for *A Summer Place* are not clearly documented, there is no question that the film was a popular success and has gained a following in the decades since its release As of this writing, the movie has an 83 percent rating with Rotten Tomatoes.

Film Facts

Director: Delmer Daves
Studio: Warner Bros.
Release Date: November 18, 1959
Stars: Sandra Dee, Troy Donahue, Richard Egan, Dorothy McGuire, Arthur Kennedy, Constance Ford
Running Time: 130 minutes
Budget and Box Office Gross: not clearly documented

9

ETHAN HAWKE AND JUDE LAW AIM FOR OUTER SPACE

MARIN COUNTY CIVIC CENTER, NORTH SAN PEDRO ROAD, SAN RAFAEL

Marin County is known for many things, most of them associated with the laid-back lifestyle of the residents of this prosperous enclave just north of the Golden Gate Bridge. It is also the location of the last design of a public building by Frank Lloyd Wright to be approved during his lifetime: the Marin County Civic Center. Today, this facility is one of the most well-known and well-visited of all of Frank Lloyd Wright's designs on the West Coast, with guided tours on Fridays every week. This "space age" site was also used in two dystopian science fiction films: George Lucas's first feature film, *THX 1138*, and the 1997 movie *Gattaca*. A third futuristic film, *DreamQuil*, was filmed there in 2024. Yet the construction of this iconic Wright creation was almost derailed before it could begin.

The hills in the eastern part of Marin County take on a golden hue for most of the year. Their soft, rounded contours sprinkled with scrub brush and clusters of live oaks rise and fall in gentle waves as they undulate across the landscape. This is the setting for the most distinctive government complex in the United States and the only government facility designed by Frank Lloyd Wright ever built. The story of how it came to be created, and the heated controversy it generated when Wright first proposed his design, is one of the most colorful and compelling stories in the history of American architecture.

In the early 1950s, Marin County's rapidly growing population was poorly served by an antiquated courthouse in downtown San Rafael and

Marin County Courthouse, with the administration wing on the left and courthouse on the right. *Photo by Joel Puliatti.*

by various county offices scattered around a dozen locations. Between 1950 and 1960, Marin County's population nearly doubled, from 86,000 to 147,000. So, in 1953, the board of supervisors began seeking a site for a new courthouse that would also include most of the other county offices. San Rafael was already an old California town by then, founded in 1850 by Yankee pioneers whose first rustic homes were clustered around the grounds of the abandoned Spanish mission San Rafael Archangel. In the mid-1950s, the hills north of the Victorian-era downtown remained largely undeveloped open land. Most of the city's business and political leaders agreed this would be an ideal location for a new civic center. On April 27, 1956, the county purchased a private ranch for $126,000 in an area called San Venetia, just east of Highway 101.

During the following year, a committee interviewed dozens of architects and created a list of twenty-six names of architects, one of them being Frank Lloyd Wright. In April 1957, four of the five supervisors met with Wright in his office in San Francisco to discuss the project, and on June 27, 1957, those same supervisors voted to begin negotiations with Wright, after they had recommended him as the architect for the project. And that's when the trouble began.

The problems that beset the project had their root in the old boy network, which had dominated Marin County politics until the election of 1955, when a more progressive group took office. The new board consisted of four men and one woman, Vera Schultz, who was to prove pivotal in the conflict over the civic center. She had been elected in 1952 and was the first woman ever to serve on that body, earning the nickname "First Lady of Marin." Vera was the most ardent backer of Frank Lloyd Wright as the architect for the new civic center and had the support of three men on the board. But the fourth, the ironically named William Fusselman, together with his ally County Clerk George Jones, did everything they could to prevent Wright from getting the commission. They came close more than once using questionable tactics in a sustained effort to derail Wright's plans and force the board to choose a different architect. If not for Schultz's unwavering support and ironclad determination in the face of such heated opposition, Wright's version of the civic center would never have been built.

Fusselman's opposition was based on several factors. At the June 26 board meeting, he accused his fellow supervisors of "crawling to Wright at the bidding of one of his vassals to bow and kiss his hand" (who this "vassal" was is not clear). He also accused them of not giving proper consideration to architects based in California. In addition, he objected to Wright's fee of 10 percent of the total construction costs, when most other architects were only charging 8 percent. In response, Planning Director Mary Summers pointed out that Wright's fee was "really quite inexpensive when you consider it includes the costs of a master plan for the site," which was usually paid separately in large government projects. And Schultz reminded Fusselman that he'd chosen not to accompany the other board members when they went to visit Wright. But Fusselman's most aggressive objections had to do with Wright's purported political

Vera Schultz. *Courtesy of Anne T. Kent California Room, Marin County Free Library.*

reputation. When four of the board members signed a contract with Wright on July 26, 1957, Fusselman refused to sign it. He soon launched a whole new line of attack, including an array of bitter, vitriolic and spurious personal accusations that nearly made Wright decide to withdraw from the deal; this has a familiar ring in today's acrimonious political climate.

The day after the four supervisors signed the contract, Wright appeared before a large crowd in a public meeting at San Rafael High School. He told the meeting they would be getting a "fresh, convenient, and beautiful civic center with plenty of parking." The *Marin Independent Journal* reported the next day that "Wright's sharp wit and caustic observations kept the crowd of about 600 applauding and laughing during a one-hour show." In his opening remarks, Wright declared, "Civilization without culture is like a man or woman without a soul. Culture consists of the love of beauty in the human spirit." Then he took questions from the audience. One man asked how he would halt the "cancerous growth of present building projects that are ruining Marin County." Wright replied, "Well, there's the atom bomb." He then launched into a tirade about utility poles and wires and the "tiny lots" that were jamming homes side by side, and added, "We've got to go out and abolish the realtor. I've hated him since the inception of my architectural career." Then he took local citizens to task for not demanding higher-quality development. "If you are up for something better—you are going to get it," adding with his characteristic arrogance, "When people go for an architect, they should go on their hands and knees as far as they can go to get the best, because the best isn't good enough." Supervisor Fusselman was conspicuously absent from this meeting, while the other board members were in attendance.

Political objections to Wright as the new civic center's architect first surfaced on July 25, 1957, when a Marin County Veteran's Service officer complained that Wright was "not fit" to design the veteran's memorial component of the civic center complex. "We don't like his war record, and we don't want his name on our veteran's memorial building," W.P. Duhamel said at a supervisors' meeting. "We think Wright is a pacifist. From what I've heard, during World War Two he had several conscientious objectors among his staff. His name was mentioned in the 1948 report of the House Un-American Activities Committee—and I would say unfavorably." But four of the supervisors ignored Duhamel and passed a resolution restating their decision to draw up a contract with Wright. Once again, Fusselman was the lone dissenter, and this would be just his opening salvo in an ugly campaign to impugn Wright's patriotism and loyalty as an American citizen.

At the next supervisors' meeting on August 2, Fusselman brought out his big guns. This meeting was supposed to finalize the decision to proceed with Wright's plans and be followed by a site inspection with Wright. Instead, it turned into a three-ring circus. Bryson Reinhardt, an American Legion member from Mill Valley, demanded to include a seven-page report in the meeting record, which accused Wright of having "a record of active and extensive support of Communist views and enterprises." The meeting erupted into acrimonious debate. The report had been prepared by J.B. Matthews, a former member of the House Un-American Activities Committee and an investigator for Senator Joseph McCarthy. Some of the allegations in the report included the charges that Wright had "expounded the Communist line on TV," praised "Sovietism" in a 1937 issue of *Soviet Russia Today*, wrote an article for the left wing magazine *The Masses*, supported the Progressive Party candidate for president Henry Wallace in 1948, was a supporter of the Cultural and Scientific Conference for World Peace in 1949 and joined the American Committee for Protection of the Foreign Born.

The first person to respond was the architect himself. He labeled the charges "ridiculous and an unjustified insult that had been buried long ago. There's no substance in that. I'm a loyal American, everybody knows it—I am what I am. If you don't like it, you can lump it. To hell with it

Site conference for the Marin County Civic Center; from right, Aaron Green and Frank Lloyd Wright, circa 1958. *Courtesy of Anne T. Kent California Room, Marin County Free Library.*

all." Then he stood up and stalked toward the exit. Supervisor Castro asked, "Do you mind?" Wright replied angrily, "Yes, I mind being insulted like this!" He continued to the exit doors and then paused, turned around and waved his cane toward the audience. "This is an absolute and utter insult—I won't be subject to it!" he thundered and stalked out through the chamber doors.

After Wright left, Vera Schultz declared that Marin County had been "humiliated" by the accusations. "This county does not look into the political beliefs of any of its employees. It is certainly inappropriate that we should subject a man of Wright's caliber to the reading of such unfounded and unsubstantiated charges." Only Fusselman demanded that the charges should be read into the meeting record, so they never were. When the meeting adjourned, the other four supervisors drove to Santa Venetia to join Wright in inspecting the site. When they arrived, they found Wright, who had calmed down by then, walking briskly up and down the hillsides despite his ninety years, scurrying all over the hilly terrain, ducking between strands of barbed wire fence and enthusiastically assessing the site. The supervisors struggled to catch up with him, and

"Beauty is the moving cause of nearly every issue worth the civilization we have, and civilization without a culture is like a man without a soul. Culture consists of the expression by the human spirit of the love of beauty.

"We will never have a culture of our own until we have an architecture of our own. An architecture of our own does not mean something that is ours by the way of our own taste. It is something that we have knowledge concerning. We will have it only when we know what constitutes a good building and when we know that the good building is not one that hurts the landscape, but is one that makes the landscape more beautiful than it was before that building was built. In Marin County you have one of the most beautiful landscapes I have seen, and I am proud to make the buildings of this County characteristic of the beauty of the County.

"Here is a crucial opportunity to open the eyes of not Marin County alone, but of the entire country to what officials gathering together might themselves do to broaden and beautify human lives."

Frank Lloyd Wright
From an address to the people of Marin County, July 1957

Frank Lloyd Wright in 1957, with a quote from his address to the citizens of Marin County. *Courtesy of Anne T. Kent California Room, Marin County Free Library.*

when they finally did, Wright was standing on top of a hillside talking to several reporters and citizens.

> *"Splendid!" Wright declared to the assembled group. "It's as beautiful as California can have." Two 15-year-old girls asked him to pose for a photo, and he happily obliged.*
>
> *"Are you going to knock these hills down?" one of them asked.*
>
> *"Not a single hill!" Wright replied, smiling enthusiastically.*
>
> *Another citizen asked if he planned to make another site visit before he drew his plans.*
>
> *"I don't have to drink a tub of dye to know what color it is," he replied.*

Two hours later, Wright was back at the old courthouse to sign the contract to design the new civic center. It called for a projected budget of $8 million (in the end, the final budget for the entire project, including the Veteran's Memorial Auditorium and the fairgrounds, came to $19,523,000). So, Wright was finally chosen as the project architect, even though Fusselman would engage in attempts to thwart its construction over the next few years. His efforts would fail, since the majority of Marin County citizens clearly supported the project.

A second public meeting was held on March 25, 1958, in the San Rafael High School auditorium, where over seven hundred Marinites had the opportunity to peruse a set of drawings of the civic center complex that had been produced by Wright's studio. The *Marin Independent Journal* ran an article the next day with a drawing of the Administration Building wing. An article in the *San Francisco Chronicle* about this meeting had this subheading: "How to put $9 million of government center into Marin's sunburnt hills so you can hardly notice it—was illustrated in San Rafael last night by Frank Lloyd Wright." At this meeting, Wright acknowledged that his estimated budget for the project had increased by $3 million from his original estimate (a common occurrence with Wright's original bids on many of his projects). But he claimed that the Administration Building could be built for only $2,750,000, or $20 a square foot, clearly an unrealistically low figure even in that era. He told reporters who were pestering him about the increased cost, "Simplicity is often expensive, you know; but in this case I think you will find it is economical." All five of the supervisors attended the meeting, and all but Fusselman expressed their unequivocal support for the project, despite the cost overruns. So, on April 28, 1958, the board voted four to one to approve Wright's plans.

When Wright died on April 9, 1959, the board of supervisors voted to continue with the project, with the Frank Lloyd Wright Foundation and Wright's associate Wes Peters as the chief architect and Aaron Green as supervising architect. They worked from Wright's own detailed drawings to carry out his design essentially as he had designed it. One revision they did make was to change the color of the roofs from gold, as Wright had desired to blend with the color of the hillsides, to sky blue after it was determined that gold paint would quickly tarnish into a dirty brown.

Fusselman and his supporters had been trying to rally grassroots opposition to Wright's plans even before he died. In early March 1959, a lengthy article in the *San Francisco Examiner* described these efforts. "A steadily growing number of Marin County taxpayers are denouncing the $13,800,000 county civic center project as 'a second Taj Mahal'—a grandiose monument far beyond the needs and financial means of the taxpayers." The article went on to explain that Wright's original cost estimate had been inflated by what many citizens considered unnecessary expenditures, such as swimming pool mounted on a hydraulic lift so it could also be used as a ballet stage, a huge artificial lagoon and $250,000 escalators. A group of forty-six taxpayers had written a letter to Governor Edmund G. Brown protesting the way the board of supervisors had approved the project and asking for an official investigation. In the end, the swimming pool, an outdoor amphitheater, a restaurant, a senior citizens center and a zoo were never built. But there was no investigation, and the project proceeded despite Fusselman's repeated attempts to derail it.

Construction on the Administration Building began on February 15, 1960. The first building completed was the post office, which opened in May 1962, and the Administration Building was dedicated on October 13, 1962. Its completion was delayed by a stop order issued in 1961 by a newly elected board in which two of Fusselman's allies had won seats. But construction soon resumed on January 17, 1961, after the *Marin Independent Journal* published the results of a poll of its readers, which showed 8,152 were in favor of completing the project and only 1,225 were opposed.

In November 1963, the board voted to commission the Frank Lloyd Wright Foundation to draw up plans for the Hall of Justice. Aaron Green designed a series of circular courtrooms, as well as moveable walls in some offices, which were not part of Wright's original plans, but his detailed plans for the jail cells did conform to Wright's concept. Groundbreaking came in 1966, with construction, supervised by Taliesin Associated Architects,

Marin County Civic Center Administration Building under construction, circa 1961.
Courtesy of Anne T. Kent California Room, Marin County Free Library.

completed in December 1969, and the building opened to the public in 1970. The dedication brochure for the Administration Building contained this statement from Wright: "We will never have a culture of our own until we have an architecture of our own. We will have it only when we know what constitutes a good building—the good building is not one that hurts the landscape, but one that makes the landscape more beautiful than it was before the building was built." Anyone who doubts the Marin Civic Center meets this standard need only engage in a simple exercise: imagine Marin County without it.

Wright's concept for the civic center was really quite simple and at the same time a stroke of genius. As he had promised the two fifteen-year-old girls the day he inspected the site, his plan called for leaving the hills intact. The main part of the complex was to be a low-lying, V-shaped set of wings, with the Administration Building in the south wing and the Hall of Justice in the north wing, joined in the middle by a shallow-domed library. These two wings branch out at about a 120-degree angle. The low-angled roofs on the two wings and the library reflect the shape of the rounded hills on which this structure is perched, so that it almost appears as part of the landscape at first glance. Thus one of Wright's largest and latest projects still conforms to his philosophy of "organic architecture." He further integrated this structure into the landscape by incorporating modified Spanish Colonial architectural features. The edges of the roofs are decorated with a repeated pattern of cutout or perforated half circles, and the walls along the upper three levels in both wings have rows of compressed arches, or arcades, reelecting the arches one sees in the covered walkways around the cloisters in California's Spanish missions. Wright also chose a golden tan color for the walls of this structure, a hue that both blends in with the hillsides and is similar to the color of adobe bricks used on many old Spanish Colonial houses. The structural walls of both wings are made out of concrete, while the roofs consist of concrete covered by a thick layer of polymer paint the color of the sky on sunny California days (a choice said to have been made by Wright's third wife and widow Olgivanna after his death).

Both the 560-foot-long Administration Building and the 850-foot-long Hall of Justice are nestled firmly into their respective hillsides, with wide, tall archways set into the ground level of each wing to allow traffic to access the ample parking lots just north of both wings. Wright kept his promise to the citizens of Marin County that his civic center would provide plenty of parking, a fact that visitors to this day can attest to, except during the Marin County Fair in July. Another distinctive feature of this main structure is the 172-foot-tall tower he placed near the juncture of the two wings. It overlooks a quiet patio with a garden and a reflecting pool with a fountain. Wright intended this spire-shaped tower to transmit music, but it was never outfitted with the required equipment for this purpose. This tower figures prominently in the film *Gattaca.* It and the adjacent library are two elements in Wright's concept of the function of a local government complex: not just to dispense justice and mete out punishment to lawbreakers but also to provide information and access to great art and knowledge, thus contributing to the wisdom of its citizens.

The interior of the Administration Building is just as distinctive and interesting as the exterior. Entering on the ground level beneath the wide archway, visitors pass through a set of bronze gates set in front of an escalator. These gates are embellished with an intricate pattern of vertical curls that resemble the fountain spray motifs often found in Art Deco buildings of the 1930s. The escalator leads to the first of the three main levels, which house the offices of the various county officials, as well as restrooms and a cafeteria. The most striking feature of the interior is the ceiling above the fourth level, which Wright designed in the form of a curved, clear glass skylight that bathes the open hallways below in natural light and allows the

Main archway of Marin County Civic Center Administration Building. *Photo by Joel Puliatti.*

Main entrance to the Administration Building, Marin County Civic Center. *Photo by Joel Puliatti.*

people working on each level below to look up at the sky above as they walk to and from the various offices. This is accomplished by Wright's use of another distinctive feature. The hallways on each level line the edges of a curved central light court, or atrium, creating a powerful rhythm of repeated ellipses. This feature resembles an elongated version of the spiral ramp beneath a central skylight at Wright's Guggenheim Museum in New York City, except that here there is no ramp, just stacked hallways on both sides of an atrium. The visual effect of this feature is quite striking, and it was used as the setting for several scenes in the movies *THX 1138* and *Gattaca*. These hallways have curved balconies along their outer edges that allow people on each level to have views of the hallways above or below them. The colors Wright used on the walls of these hallways are also visually enticing earth tones: red, gold, orange and yellow.

At the eastern end of the Administration Building, on the top level, is the entrance to the Civic Center Library, now known as the Marin County Free Library. The shallow dome of the library is painted a bright white color, and there are rounded light fixtures inserted into a gold-colored rim around the edges of the dome. A dome that is surrounded by a "ring of light" is reminiscent of the great rotunda of the Hagia Sophia church in Istanbul, albeit on a much more modest scale. The library dome serves as a visual anchor for the two main wings of the civic center. The Hall of Justice veers off from this central point in a north-northwest direction. This four-story structure is integrated at its far end into a hillside, one of the hills Wright saw on his visit to the site and promised not to knock down. Burrowed partway into this hillside, and almost out of sight from below, is the section holding the county jail. Wright took the unusual step of placing the jail on the top level of this wing so the prisoners would benefit from sunlight and fresh air during their incarceration. He explained this by saying, "There is no use putting prisoners in the basement to preserve them. I put these devils condemned to eternal servitude on top where they could observe nature." (Wright was overlooking the fact that at that time, county jails did not hold prisoners for more than one year in California.) The entire length of the Hall of Justice is reflected in a man-made lagoon that runs along the eastern edge of this wing.

The civic center complex includes several other sites that were part of Wright's original master plan. These include a U.S. Post Office, the only federal government building designed by Wright that was ever built. It is a small, round, low-lying building and sits across the access road to the south of the Administration Building. Wright also designed the county fairgrounds across the lagoon, which include an exhibit pavilion, a "children's island" and the Veteran's Memorial Auditorium. The public benefits that this unique government center has provided to the citizens of Marin County, and the

Upper hallways and skylight of the Administration Building. *Photo by Joel Puliatti.*

enjoyment that tourists and fairgoers get by visiting the main building and fairgrounds, are a testimony to Wright's vision of what a local government facility should be.

THX 1138 (1971)

This was George Lucas first feature film, released two years before his first blockbuster hit *American Graffiti*. It depicts a grim, futuristic world in which the government uses drugs to suppress human emotions, sexual intercourse and reproduction are outlawed, and robot police are deployed to control the population. The film was based on a prize-winning short feature Lucas had made while he was a film student at USC. During the year of its release, it was not a box office success, barely making back what it cost to produce and losing money for Warner Bros., according to Dale Pollock's 1983 book *Skywalking: The Life and Films of George Lucas*. And yet it did receive praise from some critics for its visual effects, due in large part to several of its scenes being filmed inside the Marin County Civic Center. However, both the storyline and dialogue were criticized by other reviewers, with Leonard Maltin calling the script "dull," and Roger Ebert declaring "*THX 1138* suffers somewhat from its simple storyline." The overall effect of the film for many viewers was to show a world of unrelenting ugliness, except for the scenes using the colorful interior of the civic center. The film's title refers to the ID number of the main character, who is played by Robert Duvall. All citizens must wear their ID number on a badge whenever they are in public.

The first scene set inside the civic center occurs eight minutes into the film, where a group of emotionally repressed citizens is shown walking along the central corridor of the Administration Building. Then the camera pans upward to the upper galleries as police observe the citizens for signs of inappropriate behavior. This is a self-contained environment where the government can easily control the actions of its citizens, in part by never letting them get a glimpse of the outside world. All the humans are bald or have closely cropped hair, including females, which is meant to make them look less sexually attractive to each other. THX 1138 works at a robot police assembly plant, and as the story begins, he is a loyal citizen who abides by the state's mantra to "work hard, increase production, prevent accidents, and be happy."

On his way home from work, THX stops at one of a series of confession booths to tell a Christ-like image named OMM 0000 about his daily concerns. When he's finished, a soothing voice reassures him, "You are a true believer. Blessings of the state. Blessings of the masses." At home, for entertainment THX watches videos of police beating lawbreakers or nude male and female actors dancing to music, then relieves his frustrations with a masturbation device. He is beginning to have strange, forbidden feelings for his roommate, a young female named LUH 3417, played by Maggie McOmie. She was assigned to him by a computer matchup. She works at a video control center with SEN 5241, played by Donald Pleasence. THX doesn't realize that LUH has been substituting his regular state-provided medication pills with her own illegal pills, which give him feelings of nausea, anxiety and sexual desire. The two roommates soon become romantically involved and end up having sex, despite the serious risk they know they are taking.

THX and LUH think no one is watching them, but they're being spied on from the video control center. Meanwhile, the couple discuss

Scene from *THX 1138*, George Lucas's first feature film, showing workers with shaved heads in the main hallway of the Administration Building of the Marin County Civic Center.

An eye-level view of the Marin County Civic Center's main hallway as seen in *THX 1138*.

not resuming their sedation medications so they can continue feeling sexual desire for each other. But SEN decides to interfere with their plans. So, he goes to THX and asks to become his new roommate as a replacement for LUH, but THX refuses. In the next scene, the central corridor of the civic center's Administration Building is shown again, in a composite image of the actual location on the right with CGI on the left. On the right side, we see the curved corners of the central galleries looking up from below. On the left, we see a pattern of metal gridwork and elevators receding into the background that is not in the actual civic center. The workers are shown walking around these structures as the robot police once again watch their every move. Soon after this scene, THX is arrested by the police for "drug evasion and sexual perversion." He is quickly tried and convicted and then punished with electric shock therapy to cure him of his deviant behavior. The second half of the film has a disjointed and somewhat jumbled storyline, which includes a car chase through the then-unfinished Bay Area Rapid Transit trans bay tube that runs under San Francisco Bay.

Director Lucas, only twenty-five at the time the film was released, was clearly trying to evoke a *1984*-style dystopian ambience with his initial feature film. But for all its visual impact, *THX 1138* doesn't quite achieve that goal. The *Chicago Tribune*'s Gene Siskel gave the film only two stars in his four-star rating system, writing, "The principle problem with this film is that it lacks imagination, the principal component of a science fiction film." But other critics lauded the film's interesting cinematic effects. The *New York Times*' Vincent Canby felt the film offered "a stunning montage of light, color, and sound effects that create their own emotional impact." The *Los Angeles Times* stated, "The real excitement of *THX 1138* is not really the message, but the medium—the use of film not to tell a story so much as to convey an experience, a credible impression of a fantastic and scary dictatorship of tomorrow." Over the more than five decades since its release, most viewers have praised the film, as shown by its rating of 86 percent on Rotten Tomatoes.

FILM FACTS

Director: George Lucas
Studio: Warner Bros.
Release Date: March 11, 1971
Stars: Robert Duvall, Donald Pleasence, Maggie McOmie
Running Time: 88 minutes
Budget: $777,777
Box Office Gross: $945,000 (initial release); $2,437,000 (worldwide theatrical total)

GATTACA (1997)

If you cast Ethan Hawke, Jude Law and Uma Thurman in a dystopian science fiction film; shoot many of the scenes in and around the colorful space age setting of the Marin County Civic Center; and add a well-written script with a compelling storyline, you're bound to create an interesting and highly original movie. That's exactly what director and writer Andrew Niccol did to make his debut feature film, *Gattaca*. The three principal actors were all in their twenties, and Hawke and Thurman had each recently achieved critical acclaim for their acting in the films *Before Sunrise* and *Pulp Fiction*, when Niccol chose them to play the starring roles in *Gattaca*. Although Law had made one other American feature film, *I Love You, I Love You Not*, this was the first U.S. film in which critics praised his performance. Although *Gattaca* was not a box office success, bringing in a total domestic theatrical sum that was barely one-third of its production budget, it received critical acclaim at the time of its release. It has since earned a rating of 82 on Rotten Tomatoes.

The premise of this film is that in this futuristic society, there are two classes of people. The privileged class are the "Valids." These are people whose parents have had their children genetically engineered before birth, to remove genetic defects, like diseases, weak bodies or mental illness. The lower class is called "In-Valids," people who were conceived through old-fashioned sexual reproduction and are prone to inherit genetic defects from their parents. This leads to a struggle by some In-Valids to find a way to enjoy the privileges of the Valids by disguising their true identities. During the opening credits, we see a young man taking genetic material from a refrigeration unit and then injecting himself with fluids. We don't yet know who he is or why he's doing this.

The film opens with the words "The Not Too Distant Future" on the screen. The Marin Civic Center first appears at the end of the opening credits. The Administration Building is seen from the lagoon in the glowing light of early evening, with the dome and the antennae tower at the far end. The building is supposed to be a command center for a space port named Gattaca from which flights to planets and moons in our solar system are launched. In the next scene, four minutes into the film, the main hallway is shown, as the man seen in the opening credits, whose real name is Vincent (played by Ethan Hawke), and Irene (played by Uma Thurman) are shown riding the escalator to an upper-level computer workroom. They do not know each other at this point and don't interact in this scene. (Many of the scenes in the movie that used the civic center were filmed at night, when all the county offices were closed.) In this scene, the distinctive curved balconies are shown from below as Vincent and Irene join a group of "elite" workers heading to their computer stations in the morning. When they get to the top of the escalator, they emerge into a wide hallway with a large porthole

Poster from *Gattaca* with Uma Thurman, Ethan Hawke and Jude Law.

Ethan Hawke in *Gattaca,* on the escalator in the Administration Building.

window on the outer wall and many smaller portholes lining the ceiling. This "room" is actually a composite image created by CGI of details from images of indoor and outdoor spaces at the Civic Center, while the main location was shot under the center arch of the Hall of Justice Wing. The portholes in the ceiling of the computer workroom at the end of this hallway were also created by CGI.

When Vincent gets to his workstation in the computer center at the end of the hallway and begins tapping at his keyboard, he is approached by the director of the command center, Josef, played by Gore Vidal, who calls him Jerome. Josef tells him he's doing outstanding work and he's still scheduled to go to Titan, one of Saturn's moons, on a rocket to be launched next week. In the next scene, Vincent is seen standing at the edge of one of the balconies looking up through the curved glass ceiling over the main hallway at a rocket being launched into outer space. Irene walks up to him and says, "Congratulations, Jerome." Then she asks if there are a dozen or so rocket launches there every day, and he replies, "Sometimes more." She reacts by telling him, "Well, you're the only one that watches them all." After she leaves, Vincent begins to recall pivotal moments from his childhood, which viewers are shown to explain his obsession with going into outer space.

His parents are then seen at a doctor's office talking about his mother's pregnancy. The doctor tells them that because they conceived their son the natural way, the tests that he has conducted reveal that the child will have a high percentage risk for several problems, including manic depression, heart failure, myopia and short lifespan. His parents tell the doctor they wanted to conceive him naturally but will make sure their next child is genetically modified to avoid such problems. Then Vincent is shown as a child at the beach, creating a chart of the solar system in the sand. We hear Vincent's narration say, "As long as I can remember, I've dreamed of going into space." His next memory is of sitting with his family at the breakfast table as he plays with a toy rocket and talks about traveling into outer space. His mother tells him to "Be realistic, Vincent," and his father says, "The only way you're ever going to see the inside of a spaceship is if you're cleaning one."

In his next memory, Vincent is shown riding a work cart dressed as a janitor with a group of other janitors as they stop at the main entrance to the Administration Building and go inside to begin cleaning the hallway. Then Vincent is seen with some of the janitors walking along the roof of the buildings at sunset as they mop the curved glass ceiling. Vincent pauses to watch as a rocket is launched, with a look of obvious longing on his face. In the next scene, Vincent is in the workroom mopping the floor around the rows of curved metal cubicles that line the room, (which were a set created for the movie).

When the memory sequence ends, Vincent decides to hire a middleman, played by Tony Shalhoub, who promises he can help any In-Valid pass as a Valid. Meeting with him in his apartment, this middleman explains that for a sizeable fee, he can connect Vincent with a Valid who is willing to let an In-Valid adopt his identity by donating his superior genetic material to an In-Valid, including hair, blood, skin and urine samples. This will help him pass the frequent urine and other genetic tests that all elite workers at Gattaca must pass in order to get hired and continue working there. Vincent agrees to pay the middleman 25 percent of his future earnings at Gattaca and meet the Valid donor. The donor is Jerome (played by Jude

Scene from *Gattaca* as elite workers head to the computer room in the Administration Building. This was a composite image created by CGI.

Scene from *Gattaca*, with elite workers going to work in the Marin CCC Administration Building.

Law) a healthy young man who was hit by a car a few years ago and is now wheelchair bound. Jerome explains that he once had dreams of being a champion swimmer, but he now wants to make some money by putting his superior genetic heritage to good use by helping an In-Valid "beat the system" and realize his dreams. The two men begin a sometimes-tense arrangement in which Jerome provides Vincent with the needed genetic material to work at Gattaca after he is hired. With his new identity, Vincent advances rapidly at Gattaca posing as Jerome, and he's soon chosen for the mission to Titan.

One day, the highly unpopular director for all the space missions at Gattaca is found bludgeoned to death on the floor of the workroom. A detective is called in to begin a murder investigation. Detective Hugo (played by Alan Arkin) orders all the employees at Gattaca to be interviewed as possible suspects, because he feels "everyone's a suspect" since the mission director was so despised by all the workers. This worries Vincent, since the mission director had tried to call off his flight to Titan on more than one occasion, giving Vincent ample motive for a violent act against him. When Detective Hugo finds one of Vincent's eyelashes near the crime scene, he has it tested and learns that there is an unidentified In-Valid posing as an elite worker at Gattaca. On hearing about this discovery, Vincent's anxiety skyrockets, affecting his work. Meanwhile, Director Josef takes Irene aside one day as Hugo's detectives are examining the workroom and asks her to help with the investigation by checking the hiring records of all elite employee to see if an In-Valid slipped through somehow, and she reluctantly agrees. Soon, Hugo matches Vincent's eyelash with an image of him as an In-Valid from old employee identity records and posts a photo of Vincent's face to every computer in Gattaca.

When Vincent goes to Jerome and says he believes he's about to be outed as an In-Valid and thinks he will have to give up his dream of going on a space mission, Jerome chastises him as a "quitter" and tells him, "Don't you get it? They don't see you anymore, they only see me." Jerome explains that's because they can't believe that an In-Valid could pull off such a switch and "beat the system." Vincent agrees not to give up and continue working at Gattaca in hopes he can still get on the flight to Titan, which is scheduled to launch in one week. The second half of the film depicts the growing friendship between Vincent and Jerome and deepening feelings between Irene and Vincent, set against the backdrop of the dangerous cat-and-mouse game of "catch the In-Valid" playing out between Vincent and Detective Hugo.

The underlying theme of how one's genetic origins affect one's identity and destiny is brilliantly portrayed in this sleeper of a movie, which has gained devoted fans over the years since it was made. It also received praise from film critics at the time of its release. Gene Siskel and Roger Ebert both gave the movie a thumbs up; Siskel said *Gattaca* had "a smart script," while Ebert wrote in the *Chicago Sun Times*, "This is one of the smartest and most provocative of science fiction films, a thriller with ideas." And the respected independent film critic James Berardinelli wrote that *Gattaca* had a "thought-provoking script and cinematic richness." The film was nominated for an Academy Award for Best Art Direction and a Golden Globe Award for Best Original Score, and Andrew Niccol won the London Critics' Award for Best Screenwriter of the Year. Not bad for the first feature film by a then little-known director from New Zealand.

FILM FACTS

Director: Andrew Niccol
Studio: Columbia Pictures
Release Date: October 24, 1997
Stars: Ethan Hawke, Uma Thurman, Jude Law,
Alan Arkin, Gore Vidal, Ernest Borgnine, Tony Shalhoub
Running Time: 112 minutes
Budget: $36 million (estimated).
Box Office Gross: $12,532,777 (U.S. and Canada);
$12,533,504 (worldwide total)

DreamQuil (2025)

DreamQuil is a psychological thriller directed by Alex Prager set in the not-so-distant future. It was filmed in 2024, using the Marin County Civic Center as one of its key locations. This film is about a woman named Carol who embarks on a virtual wellness retreat in order to get her life back on track—but with nightmarish consequences. The release date has not been determined as of this writing.

Carol, played by Elizabeth Banks, is a dissatisfied career mother who is struggling to find a real connection in her marriage to Gary, played by John C. Reilly, and to her child. Worried that she could be headed toward divorce, Carol leaps at the chance to get her life back on track by signing up for a digital wellness retreat. However, things take a sinister turn on Carol's homecoming. *DreamQuil* forces us to face the realities of our changing world and explores how the automation of society impacts our identity and reminds us of what makes us human. The film is being produced by Brownstone Productions, Patriot Pictures and Landay Entertainment.

Music Videos

In 2011, the music video for "I Need a Doctor," starring hip-hop musicians Dr. Dre, Eminem and Skylar Grey, used the exterior of the Administration Building for one of its scenes. "Weird Al" Yankovic hosted a concert at Wright's Veteran's Memorial Auditorium across the lagoon on October 2, 1999, during his "Running with Scissors" Tour. The DVD of the concert was released on November 23, 1999. On Sunday, March 24, 2024, "Somewhere Out There," a song performed by musician Glen Perry, was filmed live at the Marin County Farmer's Market on the grounds of the Marin County Civic Center.

10

THE WALT DISNEY AND ALFRED HITCHCOCK CONNECTIONS

In 1960, my family visited Disneyland for the first time. My three brothers and I could barely contain our excitement as we walked through the streets of this "Magic Kingdom" and saw all the exotic sections of the theme park that we had seen featured on the *Walt Disney Presents* TV show each Sunday evening back in Chicago where we lived. My favorite section was Tomorrowland, with its Rocket to the Moon ride and the House of the Future. This was a full-sized working model of what private residences might look like by the time my generation grew up. Having lived in Chicago all my life, I was well aware even at that young age of the fact that Frank Lloyd Wright was said to have invented the "modern house" with his Prairie-style homes in the Chicago in the early twentieth century. My father also taught me to admire Wright's Fallingwater Usonian house from the 1930s. So when we walked through Disney's House of the Future, he told me it must have been inspired by Fallingwater, and perhaps it had been designed by a follower of Wright. Indeed, many of the tourists visiting it that day commented that it could have been designed by Wright or at least inspired by his residential work.

We were all wrong, on several counts. The model was designed in 1957 by two architecture professors from MIT who had no connection to Frank Lloyd Wright. Although the design of the house emphasized clean, unadorned walls, large expanses of glass in its floor-to-ceiling windows and rooms bathed in natural light, all features pioneered by Wright, these similarities were outweighed by major differences. This house was built on a cruciform floor plan, in four separate pods extending outward from the center, contrary to Wright's use of open, free-flowing floor plans with horizontal orientation. And the most un-Wright-like feature of this house was that the walls were all made of molded plastic, a material Wright never used, since he preferred natural materials like wood, stucco and stone or concrete made from local sand. In fact, Wright once famously derided the use of plastics in residential buildings when he disparagingly referred to Dallas, Texas, as a "city made of rubber bathmats." There was one feature that was vaguely similar to Wright's Fallingwater design: the House of the Future was set on a raised foundation above a body of water, (a man-made pond that surrounded it) but it lacked the visual impact of Wright's placing his design above a rushing waterfall.

However, there *were* direct connections between Frank Lloyd Wright and Walt Disney during their careers. These two innovative geniuses admired each other's pioneering work in their respective design fields, and Wright's design philosophy did have an influence on Walt Disney's work. Although the two men had only a handful of direct contacts during the 1930s and early '40s (according to the comprehensive biography of Walt Disney by Neal Gabler), a record of what was discussed at those meetings has not turned up. Perhaps these two icons of creativity wanted to keep their conversations private. But Wright did attend a very important meeting with Disney's design staff in 1939, while Disney was working on his groundbreaking film *Fantasia*, which many film historians consider to be his masterpiece. Transcripts from that meeting have been released in recent years, and although not common knowledge among the general public, the topics discussed by Wright with Disney's staff and his opinions of Disney's work, are now well documented.

This unique meeting took place on February 25, 1939, in a projection room at Walt Disney's old Hyperion Studios in Glendale. The meeting was arranged by Disney to expose his staff to new design ideas that could be helpful in their tasks of using innovative techniques to create the kind of films that had never been produced by a Hollywood studio before. Those in attendance included Disney's top talent, story men T. Hee and Otto Englander; animators Bill Tytla, Mel Shaw and John Hubley; and music specialist Leigh Harline. Shaw later recalled what Disney's intentions were in inviting famous creative people such as Wright to give individual lectures on the creative process. "Walt was really imbuing all of us with something that made us feel we were part of a movement that could be considered a Renaissance in the animated cartoon business." Some of the extended

Walt Disney, circa 1940s. *Courtesy of Bison Archives.*

excerpts from Wright's lecture (posted on the noted animation historian Jim Kurkis's *Cartoon Research* website) provide classic examples of Wright's acerbic wit and his penchant for playing the role of iconoclast and provocateur when assessing the work of other artists.

At the beginning of the meeting, Wright showed Disney's staff his copy of a 1934 Russian animated film *The Tale of Tzar Durandai*. This film had a musical score composed by the famed Russian composer Dmitri Shostakovich, and it employed a then-new technique of combining music and animation in an abstract manner rather than the traditional approach taken by most producers of animated films. Disney was searching for a pleasing balance between music and animation as his staff worked on *Fantasia*, which would be released in 1940. He had already tapped the popular conductor and composer Leopold Stokowski to help select and direct the music for the movie's soundtrack. After screening the film, Wright launched into his lecture—and as usual, he didn't pull any of his punches.

> *Walt Disney is something unique. He is what he is. I think that he happened to stumble upon the future development of the cinema. I don't think it was his fault. He happened on it with this peculiar gift of his, which I think is precious. It shouldn't be violated. He shouldn't become too art conscious. That is what makes me feel that Mr. Stokowski is coming in here with this type of music, which is picture music, to have you extra illustrate the music. I think you should have the type of music that was in the Russian cartoon. The music was abstract, just as it was abstract drawing—the whole theme was an abstract thing.*
>
> *I was regretting that you take picture music and illustrate it, rather than doing something with music—having the two things made one. Haven't you got guys to write the music? Even though it's crude and simple, it would be good. You shouldn't take* Clair de Lune *and these things which are not good music anyway. I don't care what Stokowski says. I wish he were*

here. He knows better. He's got some Russian blood in him himself. I can't believe he would imagine that you seriously are doing your best when you are merely extra-illustrating pictorial music.

Wright's next comments revealed his oft-stated disdain for popular culture and the preferences of many of America's average citizens for traditional things:

In this film you must have seen perfect correlation between music and design. The whole thing is design—instinctive design, which is perfect design. There is no reason you boys can't do that. If you drive a modern car in front of a Colonial house, you insult either the car or the house every time you do it. There will always be people who like old-fashioned music. They are dead people. They live in the past, not in the present or the future. They are gone. We should treat them tenderly and with consideration, and have the caskets ready."

But you fellows—there has never been anything like this. You've got a clean spread. If you get it all mixed up with these sentimentalities, God help us. The more nearly you can strip the things you're doing clean, and establish this simple child-like correlation between things and make a child-like thing out of it and not get too sentimental about it, the better, I think.

There's one thing that distresses me in your productions, and I think people think the same about it—one can emphasize the senses quite with impunity. It's desirable. The moment you emphasize sensuality it becomes disagreeable. There is a touch of what I call vulgarity that creeps into your films sometimes. I guess it's box office and it gets a horse laugh from the worst elements in the audience. I think you should be a little shy of that. Old Grey Head speaking. When I was here before, I told Walt Disney that the introduction of the two condors was the thing that was, to me, the most remarkable thing of the film [referring to Disney's Snow White and The Seven Dwarfs]. *It prophesied something greater that might come. Didn't they give him the prize in the East, and didn't they mention the two condors?*

The thing you are in is as fresh as a daisy. Don't let it get bawled up with those sentimentalists. Tell Stokowski if he can't come in and write music for you that has the proper quality and appropriate to the thing you're doing you don't want him. At all. Stokowski isn't running the show, is he? Put him on the spot. When you take music as one thing, your animation is another, your story is another thing, there you've got a division that is fatal right at the beginning. It's unison between the three and making those three one that is the only road to anything you might call worth the name of art or worth the name of entertainment.

Frank Lloyd Wright, circa 1930s. *Courtesy of Hanna House Collection, sc0280, Department of Special Collections and University Archives, Stanford University.*

Next, Wright laid out his firm belief that people with superior creative talents should never try to make any art that appeals to the tastes of the masses.

> *Why have you got modern architecture today? It isn't an accident. Somebody stood there. Somebody asserted the fact of the thing. It's no different from you. We're all alike. Our reactions would be similar to almost anything. It takes a little character and guts and a stand-by to see it through. That's all. People are very much, as people, like sheep. If you begin to temporize and pat them on the back, and cater to their idiosyncrasies, you'll never get anywhere. This commercialization of things, commercialization of everything, I think that's what's the matter with the country.*
>
> *The public doesn't know what it wants. If the public is paying your bills, it's entitled to have you stand up to the thing you do because you alone know. I think you're going back on your public when you try to find out what the public wants and give it to them. No public knows. As compared to the fine thing they might have. They don't know what they miss. Explode once or twice and see what the reactions are.*

And then Wright gave this sage advice about staying true to one's vision to Disney's artists, and by extension to Walt Disney himself.

> *Don't let this "Box Office"—and this idea of what pleases people bother you. Concern yourself with the best and finest thing, by God, that you know, and do it to the top and give it to them to the hilt and you'll go places and you'll never lose."*

After Wright's lecture was over, Disney's staff ran their recently completed *Sorcerer's Apprentice* sequence from *Fantasia* for him. His reaction was not positive: "The music is all sentimental right from the beginning. It's all off key from the beginning. There's something wrong about the whole thing."

Millions of movie fans who have watched that sequence over the decades since the film was released would beg to differ. After all was said and done, despite Walt Disney's admiration for Wright's creative talents, he chose to ignore much of the advice Wright gave that day about "improving" *Fantasia.* When the film was released in 1940, after it had taken Disney's staff over two and a half years to create it, Leopold Stokowski remained as the conductor of the classical music used throughout the film, and *The Sorcerer's Apprentice* was kept as a key segment of the soundtrack. ("Clair de Lune" had already been cut by Disney from the soundtrack the year before Wright's lecture.) The movie drew a plethora of critical acclaim but did not make a profit at the box office during its initial release, which was partly due to the Second World War in Europe preventing the film from being released on that continent, which had normally been one of Disney's most lucrative markets. However, in the years since then, when adjusted for inflation, *Fantasia* has become the twenty-fourth highest-grossing film in U.S. history.

Another connection between Frank Lloyd Wright's work and Walt Disney's is the way in which Wright's architecture has influenced the design of some of the most iconic Disney sites, both during Disney's lifetime and after his death in 1966. In 1935, Wright proposed his master plan for a "perfect community," or a city of the future that would be more organized, well-run, livable and aesthetically pleasing than the often chaotic, overcrowded American cities of that era. He called his concept "Broadacre City." This was a decentralized community where most people would live in single-family homes on one-acre lots, and the economy would be based on small-scale farming and manufacturing. There would also be plenty of green spaces for these residents to enjoy. Wright created a scale model of his perfect community, which was shown in various magazine and newspaper articles.

Like Wright, Disney was critical of the chaotic nature of America's large cities. In 1966, he unveiled his own master plan for a perfect community of the future. He called it EPCOT, for Experimental Prototype Community of Tomorrow. Many urban historians have pointed out the similarities between EPCOT and Broadacre City, and Disney would certainly have been aware of Wright's detailed plans for such a community. Those similarities included a wide greenbelt with low-density single-family housing beyond it and well-planned community infrastructure. But there were several key differences. There would be a dense urban core at the center of EPCOT that would contain the main commercial and civic buildings, and no one would own their own homes or lots; they would all be tenants. When Disney died in December of that year, this ideal community was shelved, and planning for the Disneyworld theme park in Florida began. After the park opened in 1970, an extension of it called Epcot Center did finally open in 1982, but it bore very little resemblance to Disney's master plan for his vision of a perfect community of the future.

More direct evidence of Wright's influence on Disney sites has occurred in recent years. At Disney's California Adventure Park, which opened in 2001 across a large open plaza in front of Disneyland, there is an attraction called "Hollywood Pictures Backlot." The restroom facilities there were clearly patterned after Wright's Storer House, with walls covered by textile blocks with geometric decorative patterns, floor-to-ceiling windows and a flat roof. At the new Grand Californian hotel and resort that opened in 2017 next to the old Disneyland Hotel, the interior décor in many of the common spaces and private rooms was inspired by Wright's early Prairie style houses, which some historians consider to be Wright's version of the Arts-and-Crafts style. These features include: the horizontal proportions and Arts-and-Crafts hanging light fixtures of the main lobby, the unpainted natural wood walls and ceiling and light fixtures at the check-in desk, which resemble those used in Wright's Prairie style houses, and the Prairie-style wooden headboards above the beds in many of the guest rooms.

Frank Lloyd Wright's Influence on the Film *North by Northwest*

The "modernist" house seen near the end of Alfred Hitchcock's classic 1959 thriller *North by Northwest* has been the subject of speculation by fans of both Hitchcock's films and Frank Lloyd Wright's architecture ever since the movie came out, and for good reason. This house is the home of the arch villain of the film, a spy and traitor named Phillip Vandamm (played by James Mason) and was designed to reflect the height of modern chic in the late 1950s and show that Vandamm could afford such a luxurious home with his ill-gotten gains. This was a period in which what were commonly called "modernist homes" had reached a peak of popularity. The acknowledged master of this school of design was America's most famous architect, Frank Lloyd Wright. Thus, millions of people have assumed that this house was a real residence designed by Wright or that he at least had a hand in its design. The true story behind the creation of this residence is a complicated and interesting tale.

Although Wright passed away three months before the movie was released, there were several features that made the Vandamm house look as though it could have been designed by Wright or someone who had worked for him, while *North by Northwest* was in production in 1958. The Vandamm house had floor-to-ceiling glass walls along much of its two stories. Parts of the exterior walls and the fireplace in the living room were lined with rusticated stonework, similar to many of Wright's Usonian homes, from Fallingwater to the Walker House. And most Wright-like of all, the house was cantilevered

Alfred Hitchcock directing a movie, circa 1950s. *Courtesy of Bison Archives.*

out several feet over the ground below, a feature that is reminiscent of his most famous residential design, Fallingwater, which had become an iconic site by the late 1950s. However, the projecting wing was supported by two heavy metal struts, something Wright never did with his own cantilevered houses. Instead, he employed an internalized support system of prestressed concrete to support the cantilevered wings of his residences, beginning with his 1906 design for the Robie House in Chicago. The reason for the use of the metal struts was so that the film's hero, Roger Thornhill (played by Cary Grant), could climb up one of those struts in an attempt to rescue the leading lady of the movie, Eve Kendall (played by Eva Marie Saint). A prestressed concrete wing just wouldn't do.

In the film, Hitchcock placed the Vandamm residence just a short distance from the edge of Mount Rushmore, above the giant carved stone heads of four American presidents. This presented a serious problem for Hitchcock and his location crew. The area around Mount Rushmore is a national park, so they had to get permission to film any scenes on the

Cary Grant climbing the beams of Vandamm's house in *North by Northwest.*

ground above the cliffs, let alone on the cliffs themselves. But when U.S. park officials found out the script called for extensive use of both areas, they decided the risk of damage to the ecologically fragile landscape was too great and denied permission to film there, except for creating some establishing shots for later integration into the final two scenes of the movie. Thus, both the Vandamm house and the cliffs of Mount Rushmore had to be created through the use of sets and matte paintings utilizing the earlier footage of the actual sites. But a complication arose when Hitchcock had to choose who he wanted to design the Vandamm residence. Since he had decided that he wanted this house to be an ultimate example of modernist design, the logical choice would have been Frank Lloyd Wright. But this created a new problem for Hitchcock.

It was well known in Hollywood that Wright had been considered to design the buildings used in the 1949 film *The Fountainhead*, whose main character was an iconoclastic modernist architect, based on the Ayn Rand novel of the same title. But what was less commonly known was why Wright never actually designed any of the buildings depicted in that film, either for use as scale models or drawings to create sets. When the producers of *The Fountainhead* approached Wright about designing the sets, he informed them that his standard design fee was 10 percent of the budget, and not the budget for sets, but for the entire film, which was well above what the studio was willing to pay. In the case of *North by Northwest*, this would have amounted to well over $300,000 given the film's budget of between $3 million and $4 million, a prohibitive amount even for a director as successful as Alfred Hitchcock. So, when Hitchcock realized how expensive Wright fees would be, he decided to go another route. An anecdote that Hitchcock had his staff contact Wright directly about designing the Vandamm house has never been documented.

During the planning for the scene that would take place at the Vandamm house, the idea of using Wright's work to create this site was discussed by Hitchcock and his production crew. As pointed out in a 2022 article in *Vanity Fair* by Christine Madrid French, screenwriter Ernest Lehman described this house as a "sprawling modern structure in the Frank Lloyd Wright tradition set on a rise in the land at the end of a long driveway." And years after the film was released, Hitchcock told famed French director François Truffaut that this structure was actually "a miniature of a house by Frank Lloyd Wright seen from a distance." So, who *did* design the set, where was it constructed and how much of it was actually built?

Hitchcock tapped his production designer Robert F. Boyle to design the Vandamm house, and a set was built on a sound stage at the Metro-Goldwyn-Mayer studios in Culver City, California. All of the interior scenes were shot on full-scale sets of the rooms, and some sections of the exterior were also built as full-scale sets, such as the beams Cary Grant climbs up and the balcony where he looks inside to find Eva Marie Saint. The living room, a section of Eva Marie Saint's bedroom and the carport were also constructed.

Phillip Vandamm's house, as seen near the end of *North by Northwest.*

Eva Marie Saint, James Mason and Martin Landau inside Vandamm's house.

What appeared to be walls made of real limestone were mainly made of plaster. And due to the problem of glare from lighting and reflections of the film crew on plate-glass windows during filming, the large areas where the windows were supposed to be were left open instead. As many people who have visited a movie set know, many of the walls of these sets were what in the film industry are called "breakaways." They are bolted in place for some scenes and then unbolted and moved out of the way when cameras need to be moved nearer for closeups.

For the exterior views of the entire structure, Hitchcock hired artist Matthew Yuricich to create matte paintings to show the house at night from a distance. Since the entire sequence with the Vandamm House takes place at night, a large black cyclorama,or "curtain" was used to surround the various sets, so that the appearance of a dark night in rural South Dakota could be created. When the paintings of the house appeared in the film, it was clear that Wright's design concepts provided the guiding influence for this iconic film creation, with its horizontal massing, flat roofs and the integration of the building into the natural landscape. Thus, viewers of this Hitchcock classic are presented with yet another example of Frank Lloyd Wright's influence on the American film industry.

TWO THEATERS DESIGNED BY FRANK LLOYD WRIGHT

Wright designed multipurpose theaters for both of his Taliesin studios, the first one at Spring Green, Wisconsin, and the second one near Scottsdale, Arizona. These theaters doubled as live-theater performances spaces, or "cabarets" as Wright called them, and movie theaters, where Wright showed the latest films to his staff and sometimes to the public during the 1940s and '50s. The one-hundred-seat theater at Taliesin East in Wisconsin was built in 1922 as a cabaret. Wright called it the Hillside Theater. It was recently restored and reopened to the public, and films are often screened there for visitors. Future screenings can be found on the Taliesin East website, at https://www.taliesinpreservation.org/hillside-theater. This theater has a limited schedule during the late fall and winter.

The Cabaret at Taliesin West in Arizona is a much smaller space. It was completed in 1940 in Wright's desert masonry style, as were all the other structures at Taliesin West. It is partly sunken into a hillside, with the walls made from local stone. The upper portion of the wall on the left has a clerestory of windows looking out over the rest of the compound. The roof is supported by cross-strut beams and the ceiling is low, with strings of small light bulbs across it that create a festive ambience. There are built-in wall sconces along the upper right side to light the room during film showings. The seating area is long and narrow, and there are several dozen drop-leaf desks with attached seats in rows. These were used by Wright's staff when he showed films on Friday nights in the 1940s and '50s. These movies would certainly have included feature films by a prominent filmmaker like Walt Disney, since Wright admired his work, and probably films by Alfred Hitchcock as well. Today the Cabaret at Taliesin West offers an ongoing film series for the general public and mostly shows films from the period when Wright entertained his staff in this theater, such as *Meet Me in St. Louis* (1944), *Double Indemnity* (1944), *Christmas in Connecticut* (1945) and *Rear Window* (1954). The general public can book tickets online to watch movies in this unique Wright-designed "movie theater."

APPENDIX

HOW TO VISIT THESE WRIGHT BUILDINGS OPEN TO THE PUBLIC

Hollyhock House: 4808 Hollywood Boulevard, Los Angeles

Self-guided tours of Hollyhock House are offered several days per week. Go to the hollyhockhouse.org website, click on Book a Tour and read the details. Trained docents are stationed in several rooms to answer visitors' questions. Some restrictions apply. Food and beverages are not permitted inside the house, but picnicking is allowed within Barnsdall Park, which is open daily 6:00 a.m. to 10:00 p.m. Pets are not allowed inside the house, except for service animals, whose paws must be covered, and large bags are not permitted inside the house. Footwear must be flat or broad heeled, and shoe covers will be provided. Strollers will not be permitted inside the house but can be stored at the Visitor Center. There is a virtual tour that streams continually on the website, with photos of many of the recently restored rooms.

Charles Ennis House: 2655 Glendower Avenue, Los Angeles

As of this writing, the owners of the Ennis House are not able to accommodate most requests to visit their residence, since they have been receiving over three thousand requests per year recently from people who want to visit. Therefore, inquiries to the official website for the Ennis House, info@ennishouse.com, are not likely to receive a response at this time. This may change in the future, but if you send a request, a reply could take several months, and they cannot reply to many of these inquiries.

MARIN COUNTY CIVIC CENTER: NORTH SAN PEDRO ROAD, SAN RAFAEL

Docent-guided tours of the main structure at the Marin County Civic Center are given at 10:30 a.m. every Friday. Pre-purchased tickets are required to join these tours. You can go to the website https://tickets.marincenter.org and click on Buy Tickets to order. The ninety-minute tour starts in the cafeteria, room 233. It includes the Marin County Board of Supervisors' chambers and their private balcony, as well as eye-level views of the building's iconic blue roof and the custom-made furniture designed by Frank Lloyd Wright. Buy your tickets early, since the tours are sometimes booked up weeks ahead.

CABARET THEATER, TALIESIN WEST: 12621 NORTH FRANK LLOYD WRIGHT BOULEVARD, SCOTTSDALE, ARIZONA

The Cabaret Theater at Taliesin West shows classic Hollywood films about once a month to the general public so that visitors can "discover why film was so important to life at Taliesin West," according to their webpage. To book tickets for specific films, you can go to the website https://franklloydwright.org/tw-films and click on Buy Tickets after choosing a film from the list of upcoming screenings. These tickets do not include tours of the rest of Taliesin West, which can be booked by clicking on Purchasing a Tour on the same page. All the films are shown with closed captioning, and refreshments can be purchased prior to the start of these movies, when candy, popcorn, beer, wine and nonalcoholic beverages are available.

ACKNOWLEDGEMENTS

Of all the people who made this book possible, the first one I want to thank is my editor, Laurie Krill, from The History Press. She responded to my inquiry the day after I sent it and was interested in it right away. She believed in this project from the very beginning and guided me through the complex process of getting approval from her editorial board. During the writing of this manuscript, her helpful suggestions and enthusiastic comments made it a joy to work with her and improved the final text.

My friend and photographer Joel Puliatti was instrumental in providing this book with some of the best color photos of Frank Lloyd Wright buildings in California that have ever been taken. Joel supplemented his images of Wright's work from my previous book with photos that have never been published before. And his patience and skill in filing and helping me arrange all of the images for this book were invaluable. My brother John "JB" Wilson, film historian and the creator of the Golden Raspberry Foundation, was the first person I told about this project, and he was supportive of it from day one, providing much-needed research on film locations and techniques that I incorporated into this book.

Next, I want to thank Marc Wanamaker, founder of Bison Archives and one of the most respected film archivists in Hollywood. His offer to locate and send all the archival images that I requested from feature films and TV shows with scenes at Wright locations provided an essential piece of this project, without which this book would not have been possible. Libby

Garrison, the director of cultural services for Marin County, was also quite helpful in the process of obtaining other archival images from the Marin County Library at the Civic Center, as well as answering my questions about specific scenes in the film *Gattaca* and music videos that were filmed at the Civic Center. Abbey Chamberlain, director and curator for the Hollyhock House, provided the information for visitors to that iconic landmark. And Rebecca Hagen of the Frank Lloyd Wright Foundation provided help with contact information about other Wright buildings open to the public, as did Eric Rogers of the Frank Lloyd Wright Building Conservancy. And Lisa Ziven of Big Valley Pictures was helpful in providing information about the latest film to use a Frank Lloyd Wright site as a location, *DreamQuil*.

Several friends were very supportive throughout this project. Among them were some former students from my art history classes at Santa Rosa Junior College, who answered various questions I had about choices I had to make while writing this book, including Chandler Cassidy, Yohanna Pursely-Griffin, Madeline Balzarin, Alyssa Joyner and Ashlyn Cole, who created the very detailed index for this book. Linda Taylor offered her skill as a former line editor to read over the first two sections of my manuscript and correct spelling or punctuation errors. And finally, my good friend Amanda Solar read my original proposal and listened to numerous questions about issues that arose during my writing and then gave me her carefully considered opinion about how readers would react to certain aspects of the book, as well as providing critical moral support when I needed it most.

Last but not least, I'm very grateful to my wife, Ann, and my daughter, Elena, for their interest and comments during the writing of this book. Their patience with my author's need for frequent feedback at every step of the creative process and frequent questions was greatly appreciated.

Image Acknowledgements, Credits and Copyrights

Unless otherwise noted, all images are provided by Bison Archives "Editorially" under the "Fair-Use" laws with no advertising or commercial uses given or implied. Credit and copyright is acknowledged to the companies below for the use of the images in this publication.

THX 1138	1971	Warner Bros. Pictures
North by Northwest	1959	Warner Bros. Pictures
Blade Runner	1982	Warner Bros. Pictures
A Summer Place	1959	Warner Bros. Pictures
Westworld (TV)	2016–22	Warner Bros. Television
Glimmer Man	1996	Warner Bros. Pictures
Terminal Man	1974	Warner Bros. Pictures
Female (stills)	1933	Warner Bros. Pictures
Gattaca	1997	Columbia Pictures
Replacement Killers	1998	Columbia Pictures
Five	1951	Columbia Pictures
Karate Kid III	1986	Columbia Pictures
Thirteenth Floor	1999	Columbia Pictures
House on Haunted Hill	1959	Allied Artists
Rush Hour	1998	Newline Productions
Permanent Midnight	1998	Lionsgate
Cannibal Women in the Avocado Jungle of Death	1989	Full Moon Features
Star Trek: Deep Space Nine (TV)	1994	Paramount Pictures
Day of the Locust	1975	Paramount Pictures
The Rocketeer	1991	Walt Disney Pictures
Bwana Devil (poster)	1952	United Artists
Grand Canyon	1991	20th Century Fox Pictures
Black Rain	1989	Jaffe-Lansing Productions Pegasus Film Partners Paramount Pictures

BIBLIOGRAPHY

Introduction

ArchiPanic. www.archipanic.com/portfolio/frank-lloyd-wright-in-movies.
Gabler, Neal. *Walt Disney: The Triumph of The American Imagination*. Vintage Books-Random House, 2006.
Wilson, Mark Anthony. *Frank Lloyd Wright on the West Coast*. Gibbs-Smith, 2014. (This book was used for reference about the architecture of each of the eight Frank Lloyd Wright buildings described in chapters 2–9).

1. Frank Lloyd Wright's Legacy in the History of American Film

Note: The websites IMDb and Wikipedia were used for information about individual films listed in chapters 1–10. A Google search by film title takes you to the relevant pages.

ArchiPanic. www.archipanic.com/portfolio/frank-lloyd-wright-in-movies.
Architexturez. https://architexturez.net/pst/az-cf-177858.
Arch20. "5 Frank Lloyd Wright Buildings That Featured in Popular Movies and TV Shows." www.arch2o.com.
Frank Lloyd Wright Sites. "Movies Filmed in Frank Lloyd Wright Buildings." franklloydwrightsites.com/movies/.
Storer, William Allin. *The Architecture of Frank Lloyd Wright*. University of Chicago Press, 2007.
Wilson, Mark Anthony. *Frank Lloyd Wright on the West Coast*. Gibbs-Smith, 2014.

2. Vincent Price's Deceptive Invitation and Harrison Ford's Reluctant Narration

IMDb. "The Karate Kid Part III Awards." https://www.imdb.com/title/tt0097647/awards/.

Maltin, Leonard. *Leonard's Maltin's Movie Guide*. Penguin Books-Random House, 2017.

The Razzies. https://razzies.com/index.html.

Storer, William Allin. *The Architecture of Frank Lloyd Wright*. University of Chicago Press, 2007.

Wilson, John J.B., film historian. Interviews with the author, June and July 2024.

3. Ben Stiller's Total Meltdown

Frank Lloyd Wright Revival Initiative. "Wilbur Pearce House Restoration Evaluation." https://flwrevivalinitiative.org.

Gebhard, David. *Romanza: The California Architecture of Frank Lloyd Wright*. Chronicle Books, 1997.

Pearce, Konrad. Interview with the author, July 2024.

4. Cannibal Women Chase Bill Maher Around a Millionaire Communist's House

Boyle, T.C. *The Women*. Viking Books, 2009.

California Avocado Festival. "Cannibal Women in the Avocado Jungle of Death." https://thealcazar.ticketsauce.com/e/avocado-women-in-the-avocado-jungle.

Gebhard, David. *Romanza: The California Architecture of Frank Lloyd Wright*. Chronicle Books, 1997.

Secrest, Meryle. *Frank Lloyd Wright: A Biography*. University of Chicago Press, 1992.

Storer, William Allin. *The Architecture of Frank Lloyd Wright*. University of Chicago Press, 2007.

Wilson, Mark Anthony. "Frank Lloyd Wright's Other Women." *Western Art and Architecture*, October/November 2014.

5. From Westworld *to* Deep Space Nine

Archinect. https://archinect.com/news/article/12834400
Gebhard, David. *Romanza: The California Architecture of Frank Lloyd Wright.* Chronicle Books, 1997.
Home Design. https://homedesign.com/2011/05/03/millard-house-in-pasadena-by-frank-lloyd-wright.
Secrest, Meryle. *Frank Lloyd Wright: A Biography*. University of Chicago Press, 1992.
Storer, William Allin. *The Architecture of Frank Lloyd Wright.* University of Chicago Press, 2007.
Westworld Wiki. "Arnold's House." https://westworld.fandom.com.

6. Home Base of the Venture Brothers' Nemesis

Frank Lloyd Wright Sites. https://franklloydwrightsites.com/movies/.
Storer, William Allin. *The Architecture of Frank Lloyd Wright.* University of Chicago Press, 2007.

7. A Dystopian Desert Setting in the Hills Above Malibu

Frank, Jeffrey. *The Trials of Harry S. Truman*. Simon and Schuster, 2022.
Frank Lloyd Wright Revival Initiative, Projects: Arch Oboler Complex. https://flwrevivalinitiative.org.
Knight, Dorothy, and John Knight. Interview with the author, August 2013.
Storer, William Allin. *The Architecture of Frank Lloyd Wright.* University of Chicago Press, 2007.

8. Frank Lloyd Wright Designed Our House—Oops!

Johnson, Tim. Interview with the author, August 2024.
Storer, William Allin. *The Architecture of Frank Lloyd Wright.* University of Chicago Press, 2007.
Walker family personal collection, letters, 1945–1952.

Whitburn, Joel. *The Billboard Book of Top 40 Hits*. Billboard Books, 2010.
Wilson, Mark Anthony. "Frank Lloyd Wright's Other Women." *Western Art and Architecture*, October/November 2014.

9. Ethan Hawke and Jude Law Aim for Outer Space

Garrison, Libby. Interview with the author, November 2024.
Gebhard, David. *Romanza: The California Architecture of Frank Lloyd Wright*. Chronicle Books, 1997.
Marin County Library, San Rafael, file on the History of Marin County Civic Center.
Secrest, Meryle. *Frank Lloyd Wright: A Biography*. University of Chicago Press, 1992.
Wilson, Mark Anthony. "Wright's Civic Center: New Details on an Old Controversy." *Marin Magazine*, November 2014.

10. The Walt Disney and Alfred Hitchcock Connections

Animation Obsessive. "+5: Frank Lloyd Wright's Fateful Visit to Disney." https://animationobsessive.substack.com.
Frank Lloyd Wright Foundation. Taliesin West Film Series. https://franklloydwright.org/tw-films/.
French, Christine Madrid. "How One Modernist Building in Alfred Hitchcock's *North by Northwest* Changed Cinema Forever." *Vanity Fair*, September 7, 2022. https://www.vanityfair.com.
Gabler, Neal. *Walt Disney: The Triumph of the American Imagination*. Vintage Books-Random House, 2006.
Janssen, Sarah. "Top Grossing American Movies." *The World Almanac and Book of Facts 2025*. World Almanac Books, 2024.
Korkis, Jim. "In His Own Words: Frank Lloyd Wright on 'Fantasia.'" Cartoon Research, December 16, 2022. https://cartoonresearch.com.
White, Sara K. "Researching Materials." Production Designers Collective, June 12, 2016. https://www.productiondesignerscollective.org.

INDEX

C

D

E

F

G

H

N

O

P

T

U

V

W

Y

ABOUT THE AUTHOR AND PHOTOGRAPHER

Mark Anthony Wilson is an architectural historian who has been writing and teaching about historic buildings in the Western United States for over forty years. He has an MA in History and Media from California State University East Bay, where he studied under Pulitzer Prize–winning architecture critic Allan Temko. He has taught courses on art history, film history and architecture for colleges and universities throughout Northern California, including Sonoma State University, UC Berkeley Extension, San Francisco City College, Berkeley City College and Santa Rosa Community College. He has five previous books published on West Coast historic architecture. He was a guest lecturer for the Historic Real Estate program of the National Trust for Historic Preservation in cities across the United States. He wrote a column called "Owning a Piece of History" for the Knight-Ridder chain of newspapers from 1997 to 2004. His articles on history, politics and architecture have appeared in hundreds of newspapers and magazines, including the *New York Times*, *Los Angeles Times*, *San Francisco Chronicle*, *Sacramento Bee*, *Christian Science Monitor*, *USA Today*, *Marin Magazine* and *Western Art and Architecture Magazine.* Mark lives with his wife, Ann Johnson, and daughter, Elena, in Berkeley, California.

Photo by Elena Wilson.

The son of a fashion illustrator and a Sicilian pizza maker, Joel Puliatti graduated from the Parsons School of Design with a degree in illustration. He has a passion for creating custom books, filled with portraits of people and the places they love, and has been published nationally as a fine arts and architecture photographer. He collaborated with Mark A. Wilson as the photographer for their previous three architecture books. Joel lives in San Francisco with his wife, Olivia Teter, and his daughters, Jaqueline and Sophia.